# SNOWSHOEING IN THE
# CANADIAN ROCKIES

THE VIEW TO THE SOUTH INTO GLACIER NATIONAL PARK,
MONTANA, AS SEEN FROM THE SUMMIT OF FORUM PEAK.

# SNOWSHOEING
## IN THE CANADIAN
# ROCKIES

## ANDREW
## NUGARA

**RMB**
Victoria Vancouver Calgary

Rocky Mountain Books
www.rmbooks.com


Library and Archives Canada Cataloguing in Publication

Nugara, Andrew

   Snowshoeing in the Canadian Rockies / Andrew Nugara.

Includes bibliographical references and index.
Issued also in electronic format.
ISBN 978-1-926855-76-9

   1. Snowshoes and snowshoeing—Rocky Mountains, Canadian (B.C. and Alta.)—Guidebooks.
2. Rocky Mountains, Canadian (B.C. and Alta.)—Guidebooks.  I. Title.

FC219.N95 2011          796.9'209711          C2011-903317-8

Front cover photo: The beautiful environs near Crowfoot Mountain.
Back cover photo: Heading to the summit. (Photo by Bob Spirko)

Printed in China


Rocky Mountain Books acknowledges the financial support for its publishing program from the Government of Canada through the Canada Book Fund (CBF) and the Canada Council for the Arts, and from the province of British Columbia through the British Columbia Arts Council and the Book Publishing Tax Credit.


This book was produced using FSC®-certified, acid-free paper, processed chlorine free and printed with vegetable-based inks.

### Disclaimer

The actions described in this book may be considered inherently dangerous activities. Individuals undertake these activities at their own risk. The information put forth in this guide has been collected from a variety of sources and is not guaranteed to be completely accurate or reliable. Many conditions and some information may change owing to weather and numerous other factors beyond the control of the authors and publishers. Individual climbers and/or hikers must determine the risks, use their own judgment, and take full responsibility for their actions. Do not depend on any information found in this book for your own personal safety. Your safety depends on your own good judgment based on your skills, education, and experience.

   It is up to the users of this guidebook to acquire the necessary skills for safe experiences and to exercise caution in potentially hazardous areas. The authors and publishers of this guide accept no responsibility for your actions or the results that occur from another's actions, choices, or judgments. If you have any doubt as to your safety or your ability to attempt anything described in this guidebook, do not attempt it.

   Snowshoeing can be a very dangerous activity. Avalanches have injured or killed many people in the Canadian Rockies over the years. Please read **all** the introductory information in this guidebook before venturing out. Many routes described in this book require formal avalanche training and/or glacier travel and crevasse rescue training. Awareness is the first step toward ensuring your time in the mountains is safe and enjoyable.

*To Mum, Larry, Johnny, Nina, Mark, Keri and Rogan.*

THE VAST SNOWFIELDS SOUTH OF CIRQUE PEAK.

# Contents

The Trips 75

*Atmospheric views on Whirlpool Ridge.*

# ACKNOWLEDGEMENTS

My sincerest thanks to Bob Spirko and Dinah Kruze, whose interesting and well-written trip reports provided me with many routes and ideas for this book. Also to Gillean and Tony Daffern for their significant contribution to snowshoeing in the Canadian Rockies and for supplying me with plenty of route ideas. Thanks to Ferenc Jasco for his positive attitude and enthusiasm toward snowshoeing and for doing some serious trail-breaking on Mount Jellicoe and Survey Peak, and also to Dan Cote for helping to break trail on Survey. Thanks to the Rocky Mountain Ramblers and all those who post snowshoeing trip reports on the Internet. They are always excellent resources.

As usual it has been a delight to work with Don Gorman and the folks at Rocky Mountain Books.

Of course, the biggest thanks once again goes to my brother, Mark, who has always been there to help break trail, scrutinize the wisdom of some of the more dangerous routes and provide me with the best company out there.

THE BEAUTIFUL ENVIRONS NEAR CROWFOOT MOUNTAIN.

# Introduction

The Canadian Rockies in winter are nothing short of spectacular. Endless kilometres of untouched pristine terrain, strikingly beautiful mountains everywhere the eye can see, and snow and ice scenery that is guaranteed to render you breathless. Regardless of how many visits to the mountains you have made in the summer, you really haven't experienced the Rockies until you have seen them up-close during the snow season. There is absolutely no place I'd rather be on a crisp, cold and clear January day than in the Rockies, surrounded by mountains and snow, a deep blue sky above and the sun illuminating the landscape in unequalled brilliance.

Getting around the mountains in winter has unique challenges. Many choose to negotiate the landscape on cross-country or AT (alpine touring) skis, others simply go on foot, while a few more take the motorized approach on a snowmobile. Then there are snowshoes.

Snowshoeing is fun, great exercise and allows you to travel into places of surreal beauty that would otherwise be inaccessible during the months of winter and spring. The activity is growing in popularity at a phenomenal rate in western Canada.

# The Preliminaries

Before setting out to enjoy some of the most wondrous scenery on our planet, it is very important to be properly informed about snowshoes, snowshoeing and the environment you will be entering. Ignorance is not bliss here – it can be deadly! Please read **all** the preliminary information presented in the next section.

# The Changing Face of Snowshoeing

The world of snowshoeing seems to be undergoing rapid changes and shifts in focus. Historically, snowshoeing was a primarily utilitarian activity – that is, snowshoes provided an efficient means of getting from A to B when the terrain between A and B is covered in deep snow. The invention of backcountry skis and significant design improvements over the past 35 years, however, have dramatically decreased a person's need, and often his or her desire, to use snowshoes for practical travel in the backcountry. Thus, snowshoeing has started to become more recreational in nature.

Although snowshoeing as a recreational activity can be traced back to the late 19th century, it is in the mid- to late 20th century that we have seen a significant increase in this pastime. Fifty or so years ago the recreational aspect of snowshoeing may have been limited to following summer trails or exploring open areas of low-angled terrain – basically, easy hiking in the winter. However, with the recent and tremendous increase in the numbers of people taking to snowshoes, and significant technological advances in snowshoe design, snowshoers can now set their sights on far more lofty objectives that were previously the domain of mountaineers and ski mountaineers only.

# How to Use this Book and Its Focus

Snowshoeing today encompasses a staggering spectrum of levels of expertise and abilities. This is great news for the snowshoeing world, but it also means that as we push the limits of snowshoeing potential, we also must educate ourselves in all aspects of winter travel, such as avalanche awareness and the principles of mountaineering. I suppose what I'm trying to say is don't buy a pair of snowshoes, take a trip to the Hogarth Lakes one week and then set your sights on North Twin the next week. The relationship (and disparity) between these two trips might be analogous to stepping out onto the ice to play with the Calgary Flames a week after learning how to skate. (This concept is further discussed in the sections Types of Snowshoes and Types of Snowshoeing on pages 18 and 23.)

This book attempts to cover routes for all snowshoer ability levels and ambitions – from easy trips for novices to advanced outings that require mountaineering skills and may put travellers in very dangerous and potentially life-threatening situations. It is therefore very important to accurately assess your abilities and level of expertise and choose objectives accordingly.

For example, if you have not taken a course in avalanche assessment and training, only trips that are rated Easy and have no objective hazard are recommended. Chester Lake (page 192) would be a good trip for this level of expertise. If you have taken an avalanche training course, Moderate trips, such as Burstall Pass (page 202), are possible. The hardcore Difficult trips are reserved for those with formal training in mountaineering and several years of winter travel experience. Refer to Appendix A (page 321) for trip suggestions that are appropriate for your own level of experience and expertise.

As much as possible, I have tried to append Moderate or Difficult extensions to descriptions of Easy routes. This allows a beginner snowshoer to enjoy an Easy and safe trip but also see what a Moderate route looks like. It also gives the more experienced snowshoer the option to upgrade or downgrade a particular trip as conditions warrant. Example trips I recommend for beginner snowshoers are Rawson Lake and the extension of Rawson Ridge, and Chester Lake with the extension to "Little Galatea." The more experienced snowshoer may consider trips such as Burstall Pass with potential extensions to Snow Peak, or Burstall Pass Peak and Smuts Pass to "Smutwood Peak."

As you can see, this book deals with far more than just snowshoeing. Perhaps a more appropriate and descriptive title for this book would be *Snowshoeing, Winter Hiking, Winter Scrambling and Snowshoe Mountaineering in the Canadian Rockies*. That being a little cumbersome, *Snowshoeing in the Canadian Rockies* will suffice. The primary focus of this guidebook is snowshoeing.

As a cautionary note, be sure to read each route description carefully so that you are aware of any non-snowshoeing elements that may be involved. Again, refer to Appendix A (page 321) for a list of trips that only involve snowshoeing and not elements of scrambling and/or mountaineering.

## The Benefits and Advantages of Snowshoeing

Snowshoeing is great for your health and easy on your wallet, and practically anyone can do it. In addition, snowshoes can take you to places inaccessible to those on skis or foot. Provided you approach the activity sensibly, you have everything to gain by exploring the mountain environment on snowshoes.

### Health

The health benefits of snowshoeing are undeniable and profound. Snowshoeing is as good a physical workout as you can get in the winter. Calgary's Fit Frog Adventures (www.fitfrog.ca) considers snowshoeing to be a safe, cross-training, conditioning sport that provides simultaneously a low-impact, aerobic, strength-training and muscle endurance workout. As an aerobic workout, snowshoeing will help you improve or maintain cardiovascular fitness. As well, because snowshoeing uses every major muscle group at relatively high intensity for extended periods of time, it requires high caloric expenditure (400–1000 calories per hour).

Further, choosing snowshoeing as your primary winter-training activity has many benefits. Fit Frog notes that if you are a runner, substituting snowshoeing for running during the winter may improve your running fitness more than if you simply continued running through the winter. The muscles snowshoers use are the same ones used in walking and hiking hilly terrain. However, snowshoers' hip flexors may receive more of a workout and their quadriceps may get more exercise than walkers' or hikers' would; this is because of the lifting motion of each snowshoeing step. As well, snowshoeing on slopes works not only the hip flexors but also the extensors, which are important muscles for cyclists. Finally, if you choose to use poles while snowshoeing, your shoulders, arms and back muscles will also get a workout!

## Expense

Snowshoeing is a very inexpensive form of winter recreation. Assuming you already have the appropriate footwear (hiking boots), the only equipment needed is a pair of snowshoes ($100–$300) and a set of ski or hiking poles ($50–$150). That's quite a deal compared to the average $1,200–$2,000 price tag for a decent AT setup (skis, bindings, skins, boots and poles). Renting snowshoes is also incredibly inexpensive – as low as $10 a day. For those who are new to snowshoeing and unsure if they will take to the pastime on a regular basis, renting is a great idea.

## Who Can Snowshoe?

Anyone can snowshoe! Although a cliché, the saying "if you can walk, you can snowshoe" is fairly accurate. Those of us who have been walking for many years already have a huge head start in gleaning snowshoeing skills in comparison to those learning how to backcountry ski! Unlike backcountry skiing, the learning curve for snowshoeing slopes gently. While for some it may take a trip or two to become completely comfortable on snowshoes, many will learn the art within hours of stepping out into the snow. Essentially, snowshoes just make your feet bigger – quite a bit bigger – so, if you can walk with really big feet, you can snowshoe.

Of course, the "anyone can snowshoe" rule does not apply to the extreme end of snowshoeing – snowshoe mountaineering. The technical demands of this activity require formal training. This is further discussed in the section called Types of Snowshoeing (page 18).

## "TO BOLDLY GO WHERE NO MAN HAS GONE BEFORE"

The only significant advantage snowshoeing has over back-country skiing is superior manoeuvrability in tight spaces. This applies specifically to treed terrain. Weaving in and out of closely spaced trees on skis can be a nightmare – not so on snowshoes. There are some areas and peaks, such as Survey Peak, that are accessible in the winter only on snowshoes. All routes to Survey's summit require ascending a significant distance up heavily forested terrain. While this is not at all an easy task on snowshoes, it would be physically impossible on skis.

A secondary advantage to snowshoeing over skiing is the footwear required. Anyone who has scrambled or climbed wearing ski mountaineering boots knows how awkward they can be. Snowshoes allow you to choose footwear appropriate to the terrain you may encounter. For most trips hiking boots will be

A VERY SMALL SECTION OF THE HEAVILY TREED TERRAIN THAT
MUST BE ASCENDED TO GET TO THE SUMMIT OF SURVEY PEAK.

enough. However, mountaineering boots are certainly preferable for some trips.

Another small advantage snowshoes have over skis is that they are less susceptible to damage when on rocky terrain. Naturally, it is strongly recommended that you remove your snowshoes when snow has given way to rock or if there are unavoidable rocks protruding from the snow. However, if these rocky sections are short-lived, the effort of taking your snowshoes off and then putting them back on minutes later may not be worth it. Stepping carefully should be enough to avoid any damage to your shoes.

# Types of Snowshoeing

Since there are three types of snowshoes, most sources divide snowshoeing into three categories – racing, recreational and mountaineering. Although the racing category involves just that, racing on snowshoes, the components that mark the differences between recreational snowshoeing and snowshoe mountaineering bear some description. The difference between these latter two categories is so great that, in reality, at least one more category in-between them is warranted. Lacking this fourth category, however, a thorough description and explanation of both recreational snowshoeing and snowshoe mountaineering, and the deficiencies inherent in their categorization, will have to suffice.

For example, compare a recreational trip, such as Chester Lake, to a mountaineering trip like Mount Jellicoe. Anyone with snowshoes, a couple of hours to kill and a modicum of motivation and physical fitness can make it to Chester Lake and back. By contrast, an ascent of Jellicoe requires glacier travel for the approach (and the requisite knowledge and skills related to crevasse rescue), crampons and an ice axe for the main ascent slope (and the requisite knowledge of how to use these tools), possibly belayed climbing on the exposed and corniced summit ridge (and the requisite ... you get the point!), 12 to 14 hours to complete the trip – a heck of a lot more than a modicum of motivation and physical fitness.

Between Chester Lake and Mount Jellicoe sit a huge group of trips that are more serious in nature than Chester but require far less technical skill than Jellicoe. The extension from Chester Lake to the summit of "Little Galatea" would be an example of a trip that falls on the number line somewhere in between recreational snowshoeing and snowshoe mountaineering. See below for the distinct manner in which I have chosen to categorize trips in this book as either recreational or mountaineering. But first, snowshoe racing.

## Snowshoe Racing

If you prefer running to walking, snowshoe racing may be to your liking. Official races put snowshoeing into a competitive venue. However, a rapidly increasing number of people are now running in snowshoes in the same way they would run without them: purely for exercise and to maintain good muscular and cardiovascular health.

Racing snowshoes are very light and small. They are designed specifically for running on groomed trails and are therefore inadequate for backcountry travel.

## Recreational Snowshoeing

For the purposes of this guidebook, the term "recreational snowshoeing" covers everything that doesn't require use of a rope,

*THE RECREATIONAL SNOWSHOEING ELEMENT OF THE SURVEY PEAK ASCENT AND A RARE WINTER RAINBOW IN FRONT OF MOUNT MURCHISON.*

either for glacier travel or for belayed climbing. The term "recreational" here does not imply any particular level of ease or safety. Stoney Squaw Mountain and Mount Lineham both fall into the recreational category, yet the former is very easy and free of danger (objective hazard), while the latter is quite difficult and strenuous and puts you directly on or very close to dangerous avalanche slopes. Don't get lulled into a false sense of security because you are a "recreational snowshoer." The overwhelming majority of trips described in this guidebook fall into this category, which encompasses a wide range of skills and abilities.

## Snowshoe Mountaineering

Although the broadest definition of "mountaineering" is the activity of climbing a mountain, today it is generally accepted that mountaineering is the activity of climbing which requires technical skill and gear. Ropes, belaying, glacier travel and rescue are a few items associated with mountaineering. Crampons and ice axes also fall into the category of mountaineering tools, since the use of both requires some degree of technical knowledge and skill.

Snowshoe mountaineering is the cousin to ski mountaineering. It is unlikely that this form of snowshoeing will ever become popular, as most will choose the speed and efficiency of ski mountaineering over its more strenuous and laborious snowshoeing counterpart. However, for those who are lacking the requisite skiing abilities and/or the necessary alpine touring gear, and also for those who enjoy snowshoeing and want to take the activity to its highest level, snowshoes do offer a way for all to venture into terrain usually reserved only for those on skis. The visual and emotional rewards of completing a difficult trip on snowshoes are phenomenal; the price – endless hours of gruelling and physically taxing snowshoeing. Most mountaineering

BLACKFOOT MOUNTAIN IN GLACIER NATIONAL PARK, MONTANA. THE PAYOFF FOR MOUNTAINEERING CAN OFTEN BE SCENERY LIKE THIS.

trips on snowshoes push participants to, and perhaps beyond, their physical limits.

Snowshoe mountaineering is the most extreme of snowshoeing activities and requires participants to be fully trained in mountaineering skills like glacier travel, crevasse rescue, ice-axe arrest, belayed climbing, anchor building and all other associated skills.

The mountaineering aspect of snowshoeing refers specifically to glacier travel. Snowshoers must rope together in exactly the same way ski mountaineers do when travelling on a glacier and be prepared to arrest someone who falls into a crevasse and then extricate them from the hole if necessary. However, when not on a glacier, using a rope while wearing snowshoes is a mountaineering no-no. If the terrain requires belayed (roped) climbing, it is also terrain that is too serious to have something as unwieldy as snowshoes on your feet.

Obviously, when ascending very steep snow slopes (35° and above), you must replace your snowshoes with crampons and an ice axe. Taking an involuntary glissade wearing snowshoes is a worst-case scenario. The snowshoes will not release from your feet (like skis do) and, in a serious glissade, may cause major damage to your legs, knees, ankles and other body parts, not to mention death! For slopes up to 35°, you will want a snowshoe with aggressive foot and heel crampons, and possibly side crampons. Solid foot bindings that do not slip are also important.

It should be abundantly clear that the first step to becoming a snowshoe mountaineer is to seek formal training. There are many reputable companies and individuals – Yamnuska Mountain Adventures, Peter Amann, and TryThat – that offer excellent hands-on courses. I recommend the Snow and Ice Long Weekend course for everyone engaging in any form of mountaineering. You won't learn a thing about snowshoeing at this course, but that is not the focus. (To date, I have yet to hear of anyone offering a snowshoe mountaineering course.) What you will learn is how to move while roped together on low-angled snow and ice, walk with crampons, self-arrest with an ice axe and perform crevasse rescue, as well as many other tidbits about winter travel in the mountains. These elements of mountaineering may not at first appeal to the average snowshoer, but – and I'm sure many will agree – the mountains have a sneaky way of infecting those who dare enter their realm. It's a most pleasant virus to succumb to! Today Chester Lake may satisfy your ambitions, but tomorrow you may want to be part of the first group to stand atop North Twin with snowshoes on your feet.

THE MOUNTAINEERING ASCENT OF THE NORTH TOWER OF MOUNT SASKATCHEWAN. NOTE THE ROPE, CRAMPONS AND ICE AXE.

In conjunction with a mountaineering course, it is essential to take a basic avalanche safety course – Avalanche Safety Training (AST 1). Specific companies that offer these courses are listed in the avalanche section on page 41.

## TYPES OF SNOWSHOES AND BUYING SNOWSHOES

Snowshoes have evolved considerably since the early days of wooden frames bound together with animal-hide webbing. Today's snowshoes are lightweight, extremely durable and easy to put on and take off. They have superior traction and can be used to ascend steep slopes that would have been impossible with older-style snowshoes. The types of snowshoes available are categorized according to the types of snowshoeing described above. For example, racing snowshoes are small and light. They are designed to allow you to run in your natural stride. Racing snowshoes are not appropriate for trips in this book.

## RECREATIONAL VS. MOUNTAINEERING SNOWSHOES

In general, recreational snowshoes are fairly big and may or may not have crampons or other traction devices. They are designed for gentle to moderate terrain. This type of snowshoe is well suited for trips that are rated "very easy" and "easy" in this book. There are many different styles of recreational snowshoes. Choosing the one that suits your needs is best done by going to a reputable outdoors store and talking to a knowledgeable staff person.

Mountaineering snowshoes are designed for mountaineering. They can be large, but recent advances in design are allowing for smaller and therefore more manoeuvrable models. Mountaineering snowshoes often have double bindings, heel lifts and very aggressive traction and crampon systems.

It is easy to get bogged down and confused when trying to choose a pair of snowshoes. Some people will buy both a recreational pair and a mountaineering pair and then just use the set appropriate for the trip they are taking. In my opinion, the process of purchasing snowshoes can be even simpler: rent a pair of recreational snowshoes (very inexpensive) and go on several easy trips to try out the activity. Chester Lake and Rummel Lake are both great places to start. If snowshoeing appeals to you and you know you will be doing more of it, spend the money and buy one pair of high-quality mountaineering snowshoes. The advantage of mountaineering snowshoes is that they are appropriate for every type of terrain. My MSR Lightning Ascent snowshoes have tromped around the easy, flat environs of Hogarth Lakes, taken me up 35° slopes on Emerald Peak and also performed magnificently on longer treks such as Mosquito Mountain. I have never completed a trip with them and then said, "That was too much snowshoe for the terrain."

## FOOTWEAR

Buying appropriate footwear for snowshoes is an easier activity than buying snowshoes, because snowshoers most frequently use regular hiking boots. Be sure your boots have been thoroughly treated with a water-resistant barrier. Since the average air temperature you'll experience on most snowshoeing trips is considerably lower than the same trip in summer, keeping your feet warm is paramount. Buying hiking boots that are a half size or even a full size too big is often an effective strategy for dealing with cooler temperatures. The extra space in the boots allows you to wear two or even three pairs of socks, if necessary. For temperatures ranging from −5°C to −20°C, I will often wear a thin pair of liner socks and one or sometimes two pairs of thick wool socks. This combination always keeps my feet warm, and I have, not once, developed blisters or suffered other foot irritations. Make sure that your socks aren't too tight. Tight socks constrict blood flow to your feet and soon lead to cold feet. Good quality, flexible (hinged) crampons – a necessity for those who want to do snowshoe mountaineering – are available to fit most types of hiking boots.

When the temperature drops below −20°C, hiking boots may not be enough to keep your feet warm. In this case, footwear designed specifically for colder temperatures may be necessary. Baffin makes boots that are rated to −50°C. Should the temperature ever plummet to those kinds of levels, I personally have no

*WEARING MY BAFFIN BOOTS WITH SNOWSHOES
ON A VERY COLD DAY IN JANUARY.*

intention of stepping out of the house, let alone traipsing around the mountains. However, it is comforting to know that if you do, your feet will be well protected. The weakness of these boots is that they are often too big to take crampons. As such, you may be limited to trips of a less serious nature.

Another option for footwear for the extreme snowshoer is mountaineering boots. From light mountaineering boots to double plastic boots, snowshoes will accept them all. For steep snow and ice and more technical terrain, where crampons and an axe are necessary, this type of boot is definitely the best choice.

However, the overwhelming majority of trips in this guide-book can be comfortably completed wearing hiking boots. You should wear gaiters with all types of snowshoeing footwear except for the high Baffin boots (or boots similar to Baffins).

DOUBLE PLASTIC MOUNTAINEERING BOOTS WERE A GOOD CHOICE
FOR THIS ASCENT OF MOUNT ST. NICHOLAS IN EARLY JANUARY.

## ADDITIONAL EQUIPMENT

On the easiest snowshoeing trips you usually only need a pair
of snowshoes. Even on these simple outings, however, you may
appreciate having additional equipment, namely poles. If you
have more serious objectives in mind, you will require avalanche
gear and mountaineering equipment. Expect your backpack to
be significantly heavier for difficult trips! Be sure to check the
Additional Equipment list provided for each trip mentioned in
this book before you set out. There are valid arguments for taking as little additional equipment as possible, but personally I
think too much equipment is better than too little. The 10-metre
rope that permanently resides at the bottom of my backpack has
come in handy on more than one occasion.

# POLES

Ski poles or trekking (hiking) poles with baskets are essential for all snowshoers. Even on "very easy," flat terrain, poles have their purpose. Primarily, poles are used for stability, balance and

*ABOVE: POLES USED FOR BALANCE AND STABILITY ON STEEPER TERRAIN. BELOW: WITH MOUNT OUTRAM IN THE BACKGROUND, MARK AND DAN DEMONSTRATE THEIR FLAWLESS TECHNIQUE!*

support. To use a crude but somewhat accurate analogy, poles turn a biped into a quadruped. In the same way fallen skiers use their poles as leverage to regain a standing position, so can snowshoers use a similar technique, though it is not as difficult.

Poles can also be used as probes when near cornices, for glacier travel and, most important, to help assess the nature of the snowpack (see the section on avalanches, page 41).

## CRAMPONS

Whether or not you carry a pair of crampons in your backpack, very much depends on what you are looking for in a snowshoe trip. If you prefer to stick to the suggested route, note that only trips listing crampons and an ice axe in the Additional Equipment section of the route's description will require them. However, if you know you might leave the suggested route to go exploring, it is a good idea to pack a set of crampons and the accompanying ice axe.

Even the most aggressive set of snowshoe crampons is no substitute for the real thing. Foot crampons give unmatched control and stability on steep snow and ice. This reason alone is enough to guarantee that crampons will find their way into my backpack on almost every snowshoe trip I take.

Going to MEC, purchasing a set of crampons and then throwing them into your pack until they are absolutely needed is not the right way to do things, however. Test them out; learn how to walk with crampons on very low-angled terrain. The adjustments you must make are minor but important. You have to get used to walking with your feet wider apart than normal. Crampons will shred gaiters and clothing on the inside of your leg (not to mention skin and flesh if they get in the way!).

You must learn specific crampon techniques, such as flat-footing and front-pointing, if you plan on doing any of the "extreme" trips in this guidebook. Pick up Don Graydon and Kurt Hanson's

*Mountaineering: The Freedom of the Hills* or Craig Connally's *The Mountaineering Handbook* to learn more about these important techniques.

## Ice Axe

Note that the word "crampons" practically always appears alongside the words "ice axe." Like Starsky and Hutch (I'm dating myself here!) this pair is inseparable. If you have crampons on your feet, an ice axe should be in your upslope hand. It is interesting to note that the converse is not always true. Ascending a snow slope with an ice axe but no crampons is a perfectly acceptable practice in many cases.

Correctly using an ice axe is a skill that you must learn and then practise. Using an ice axe to thrust into the snow for support and to prevent an involuntary glissade is pretty straightforward. Ice axe self-arrest, should you take an involuntary glissade, is far from straightforward. Professional training is strongly recommended for anyone planning to use an ice axe. The Snow and Ice Long Weekend course referred to earlier provides a perfect introduction to learning ice axe skills, as well as many others, should mountaineering become part of your repertoire.

AN EXAMPLE OF TERRAIN ON WHICH AN ICE AXE AND CRAMPONS ARE PREFERABLE TO SNOWSHOES.

## Avalanche Gear

Please see the section on avalanches (page 41) for more information on what to pack in case of avalanche.

## Climbing Gear

If you take climbing gear with you on a trip you should know how to use it. Typically, on routes where climbing and mountaineering skills are or may be put to use, we will take 60 metres of rope, 10 metres of cord, 6–8 slings, an assortment of locking and non-locking carabiners, a belay/rappel device and occasionally a few pieces of rock gear (cams and nuts). Of course, harnesses and helmets are mandatory. It is essential to undergo specific training for using the aforementioned equipment, especially in winter conditions. Setting up belay stations, rappel stations and anchors in the winter can differ substantially from the same activities performed in summertime.

## Clothing

Clothing doesn't really qualify as additional equipment, unless of course you usually go out naked, but this is a good place to talk about the specific kinds of clothing you will need when snowshoeing.

Dressing in layers is the key to being comfortable outside in the winter months. Wool and synthetic materials such as polypropylene work best. Most people wear a base layer, a mid- or insulation layer and a waterproof and breathable outer layer.

When travelling outdoors in the cold months, you can never take too much extra clothing with you. Though impractical to take a spare of everything, your backpack should at least have one or two pairs of extra socks, an extra top layer and extra gloves. A balaclava or equivalent is also essential to have. When preparing for a trip, I often ask myself: Will the contents of my pack allow me to survive should I be forced to bivy overnight?

*YOU NEED TO BE PREPARED. AN HOUR BEFORE MY ICICLE EYEBROWS FORMED, THE SKY WAS CLEAR AND THE TEMPERATURE QUITE MILD.*

When considering clothing, it is also important to remember that even if the forecast calls for a warm, windless day, conditions can deteriorate very quickly and without warning. You must be prepared for anything. The clothing contents of my backpack are usually the same whether the forecast low is −5°C or −30°C.

Also note that high and low temperatures in weather forecasts are for the valley bottoms. Expect the temperature on a summit to be significantly colder than what has been predicted for the valley. A windy summit can exacerbate already low temperatures to an alarming degree.

When travelling in cold temperatures, it is important to keep sweating to a minimum or completely avoid it if possible. Accumulated sweat can lead to hypothermia when you slow down or stop.

The sweat cools very rapidly and can cause your body temperature to do the same. Stopping and taking the time to remove or add layers of clothing when necessary is key to safe winter travel.

## SUNSCREEN AND SUNGLASSES

Finally, don't forget to pack a tube of sunscreen with a high SPF (I use a 60) and a good pair of sunglasses that have 100 per cent UV protection. The sun's rays reflecting off snow can be intense. Getting a serious sunburn or burning the corneas of your eyes happens more easily than you might think.

# THE SNOWSHOEING SEASON

Snowshoeing season in the Canadian Rockies usually starts in December and ends in mid-May. The earliest snow of the season, in October and November, is often not consolidated enough to make snowshoeing worthwhile. Of course, unconsolidated snow can persist during any month of the season; it all depends on the prevailing weather. Objectives in the Front Ranges, where the snow may not be as deep, can provide decent day trips during these months. Expect to be carrying your snowshoes on your backpack for long stretches.

That said, the Rockies' snowpack in December and into January is typically a tough one to snowshoe on. Powdery, unconsolidated snow offers little to no support, even for snowshoes. As such, expect trail-breaking during this time to be physically taxing. Again, the Front Ranges may be your best bet. Also, objectives along Highway 742 will start to see some traffic at this time of year, and you may even find a fully broken trail!

Late January and February often see the snowpack gain strength, as the melt–freeze cycle runs its course. By late February, hopefully you will experience a significant decrease in the post-holing ordeals so common in December and January.

Reduced hours of daylight will limit you to shorter trips, but most locations in the Rockies should be ready for snowshoes.

March and April are best months. The snowpack at this time is usually strong and supportive, daylight hours are a little longer, temperatures are milder (although above treeline you can still expect to encounter brutally cold conditions), and trails have already been broken and reinforced. Plan to try some longer trips in these months. By April you will probably be looking at objectives farther west, as warm spring weather will often put an abrupt stop to snowshoeing in the Front Ranges. The warmer temperatures associated with daytime heating also mean that you have to be more aware of afternoon avalanches.

May can also be an excellent month for snowshoeing. Areas around the Continental Divide are often still lying under a substantial layer of snow. Head up the Icefields Parkway to visit areas such as the Wapta Icefield or objectives on the east side of the parkway. Isothermal snow could be your greatest nemesis on May trips. This condition occurs after repeated melt–freeze cycles, which cause the temperature of the whole snowpack to be consistent (0°C), thereby making the snow weak and unsupportive. As well, snow that is supportive in the morning can be soft and slushy in the afternoon. At this time of year, even if your snowshoes end up on your backpack instead of your feet, it's still a good idea to take them along and hope for decent snow.

You are really pushing things, however, if you pack your snowshoes when you head out to the Rockies in June. Still, it is possible in certain years and certain areas to find snowshoeing conditions in late spring. Expect your snowshoes to spend most of the trip affixed to your backpack. Areas farther west will be your best bets. The valley north of Mount Saskatchewan often holds a decent amount of snow well into June.

# Ratings

Guidebooks, regardless of whether they're on rock climbing, ice climbing, scrambling, skiing or snowshoeing, usually include difficulty ratings in trip descriptions. Giving a trip a rating is often a very subjective and dubious process. Although rating easy snowshoeing trips that have no objective hazards can be very straightforward, rating difficult trips that come with hazards (i.e., avalanches, rock falls and inclement weather) is an activity fraught with uncertainty because avalanche conditions are unpredictable and can change from day to day. For example, a trip that is rated "difficult, with considerable objective hazards" may be completely innocuous in the right conditions and pose little danger. To be safe, when rating the trips with potential hazards in this book I always considered them in their most dangerous state.

Following is the rating system used in this book, as well as the criteria I considered when rating the trips:

1. Very Easy – gentle grades with little, if any, steep terrain; short and not physically strenuous; minimal to no objective hazards. Examples are Stoney Squaw Mountain and Hogarth Lakes.

2. Easy – gentle grades with sections of steeper terrain; longer and more physically strenuous than "very easy" trips; minimal to no objective hazards. Examples are Chester Lake and Sawmill Loop.

3. Moderate – steeper terrain and longer trips that may require travel below, across or up avalanche slopes. Examples are Mount Fortune and Burstall Pass.

4. Difficult – steep terrain up to 35° and/or very long distances to travel; may require ascending or traversing avalanche slopes, exposure to runout zones, and/or glacier travel.

*Difficult trips should only be undertaken by people with mountaineering knowledge and experience.* Examples are Mount Jellicoe and Snow Peak.

Further to the four difficulty ratings above, I have also included a sub-rating system that will help you to determine a trip's level of avalanche danger. One of three hazard ratings is thus given to each trip: low, moderate or high. The hazard rating should be considered in conjunction with the avalanche danger rating of the given day you are going out. The avalanche danger rating can be found in the avalanche bulletin found on the Canadian Avalanche Centre's website, at www.avalanche.ca. The table below can also assist you in determining the overall risk level for a given day. It is derived from Frank Baumann's informative article "Snow Avalanche Risk Management" on the *Bivouac* website, www.bivouac.com [subscription required].

|  |  | HAZARD | | |
|  |  | 1 LOW | 2 MODERATE | 3 HIGH |
|---|---|---|---|---|
| DANGER RATING | 1 LOW | 1 | 2 | 3 |
|  | 2 MODERATE | 2 | 4 | 6 |
|  | 3 CONSIDERABLE | 3 | 6 | 9 |
|  | 4 HIGH | 4 | 8 | 12 |
|  | 5 EXTREME | 5 | 10 | 15 |

To use the table, determine the avalanche danger for the day and region from the avalanche bulletin and multiply it by the hazard level in the route description. A value from 1–5 is low risk, 6–10 moderate risk, and 11–15 high risk. After assessing the odds, it's up to you to decide what level of risk is acceptable to you. Remember that these are general guidelines and should never be a substitute for common sense and/or good judgment.

## The Avalanche Bulletin

The Canadian Avalanche Centre's avalanche bulletin is a critical tool for all kinds of backcountry travel. As previously mentioned, www.avalanche.ca provides frequently updated reports for most areas of the Rockies and Columbia Mountains as well as other areas in Alberta and BC. Checking the reports for the area you will be visiting several days in advance *and* on the day of the trip is an integral part of backcountry trip preparation.

Checking the rating for the day of your trip is not enough. After looking at the rating, consider the thorough discussion that appears below the rating chart. It is imperative that the backcountry traveller carefully read this synopsis. It gives detailed information on the snowpack and any potential problems that could arise from recent or forecasted precipitation, temperature changes, wind loading, PWLs (persistent weak layers) and other factors that have an impact on the stability of the snowpack.

Reading these informative reports is a terrific learning experience in itself. Anyone going to the mountains regularly can learn a tremendous amount from studying the reports and how they change from day to day.

## ATES (Avalanche Terrain Exposure Scale)

The ATES rating system is another invaluable tool for those venturing into the backcountry. It is to be used in conjunction with online avalanche bulletins and the hazard and difficulty ratings given in this guidebook. ATES evaluates the angle and shape of the terrain in question to determine the potential for avalanches and their relative severity. The strength of ATES lies in the fact that terrain rarely changes, whereas snow conditions change daily and even hourly. For example, barring a huge natural disaster, such as an earthquake, a 40° slope will always be a 40° slope. Put some snow on that slope and it now has avalanche potential. An

ATES rating helps backcountry travellers who will be on a particular slope and/or exposed to a slide from that slope.

The ATES descriptions below are taken from the Government of Alberta's Tourism, Parks & Recreation website.

| DESCRIPTION | CLASS | TERRAIN CRITERIA |
|---|---|---|
| SIMPLE | 1 | Exposure to low angle or primarily forested terrain. Some forest openings may involve the runout zones of infrequent avalanches. Many options to reduce or eliminate exposure. No glacier travel. |
| CHALLENGING | 2 | Exposure to well-defined avalanche paths, starting zones or terrain traps; options exist to reduce or eliminate exposure with careful routefinding. Glacier travel is straightforward, but crevasse hazards may exist. |
| COMPLEX | 3 | Exposure to multiple overlapping avalanche paths or large expanses of steep open terrain; multiple avalanche starting zones and terrain traps below; minimal options to reduce exposure. Complicated glacier travel with extensive crevasse bands or icefalls. |

In addition to the chart's ratings, ATES describes the necessary levels of experience for each class of terrain.

Simple, or Class 1, terrain requires common sense, proper equipment, first aid skills and the discipline to respect avalanche warnings. Simple terrain is usually low avalanche risk, ideal for novices gaining backcountry experience. Trips to Class 1 areas may not be entirely free from avalanche hazards, and on days when the avalanche hazard is rated "high or extreme" you may want to rethink any backcountry travel that has exposure to avalanches and stick to official trails.

Traversing challenging, or Class 2, terrain requires skills to recognize and avoid avalanche-prone areas – big slopes exist on trips to Class 2 areas. You must also know how to understand the avalanche bulletins, perform avalanche self-rescue and basic first aid, and be confident in your routefinding skills. You should take an Avalanche Safety Training course (AST 1) prior to travelling over this type of terrain. If you are unsure of your own or your group's ability to navigate through avalanche terrain, consider hiring a professional, ACMG-certified guide.

Finally, those who choose to travel through complex, or Class 3, terrain should be a strong group with years of critical decision-making experience in avalanche terrain. There can be no safe options on these trips, forcing exposure to big slopes. As a minimum, you or someone in your group must have taken an Avalanche Safety Training course (AST 2) and have several years of backcountry experience. Be prepared! Check the avalanche bulletins regularly and ensure everyone in your group is up for the task and aware of the risk. Class 3 is serious country – not a place to consider unless you're confident in the skills of your group. If you're uncertain, consider hiring a professional ACMG-certified guide.

In this guidebook, ATES ratings are provided for those trips that have been given a grade by Parks Canada. The remainder of the routes simply receive a Hazard rating. The following formula represents the general rule followed in this guidebook:

Low = ATES 1
Moderate = ATES 2
High = ATES 3

Using the ATES rating, the Hazard rating and the avalanche bulletin in planning a trip will ensure you are fully aware of the dangers you may face out there. Unfortunately, nothing can completely guarantee your safety, but these resources are definitely the first step in becoming aware of and minimizing the dangers.

# Avalanches

**This is the most important section of this book.** Anyone venturing out into the mountains from October to May, or in any month for that matter, needs to be fully aware of the dangers avalanches present. While snowshoers represent a very low percentage of those caught in avalanches, this obviously is in part because snowshoers have not typically exposed themselves to avalanche terrain. The increasing popularity of the activity, and books such as this one, will invariably have an impact on the statistics.

Gaining avalanche awareness can come in three ways: reading books, taking courses and gaining hands-on experience. All three are necessities, however, hopefully for everyone, the first two will precede the latter. The information presented over the next few pages is a *Coles Notes* version of avalanche awareness and by no means should replace acquiring a reputable book on the subject and also taking an Avalanche Safety Training course (AST 1). There are many experts who have written such texts. Recommended books include:

1. Tony Daffern, *Backcountry Avalanche Safety for Skiers, Climbers, Boarders and Snowshoers* (Calgary: Rocky Mountain Books, 2009).
2. Jill A. Fredston and Doug Fesler, *Snow Sense: A Guide to Evaluating Snow Avalanche Hazard* (Anchorage: Alaska Mountain Safety Center, 1999).
3. Bruce Jamieson, *Backcountry Avalanche Awareness* (Revelstoke: Canadian Avalanche Association, 2000).
4. Sue A. Ferguson and Edward R. LaChapelle, *The ABCs of Avalanche Safety* (Seattle: The Mountaineers Books, 2003).

At the time of writing, the following avalanche awareness courses are offered in the Calgary, Edmonton, Canmore and Banff areas:

1. Yamnuska Mountain Adventures – www.yamnuska.com/avalanche-courses/

2. Cirrus Alpine Guide – www.cirrusalpineguides.com/safety
3. The University of Calgary – www.calgaryoutdoorcentre.ca/avalanche-safety
4. Rescue Dynamics – www.rescuedynamics.ca/
5. On Top Mountaineering – www.ontopmountaineering.com/
6. Mountain Skills Academy – www.mountainskillsacademy.com/avalanche-safety-courses

If you haven't already done so, please investigate some or all of the above books, websites and courses.

## Types of Avalanches

There are four types of avalanches to be concerned about when out in the backcountry: loose snow, slab, cornice collapse and ice avalanches from the collapse of seracs. All are serious enough to cause severe injury or death. Slab avalanches are the most notorious for snaring backcountry travellers.

### Slab Avalanches

Slab avalanches are generally considered to be the most dangerous type of avalanche because of their frequency, not necessarily their destructive force. However, they can obliterate everything in their path. Slab avalanches occur when a cohesive slab of snow breaks away from the snowpack. While going down, the slab will break up into smaller pieces and may also trigger other nearby slabs to slide.

The slab can range in depth from a few centimetres to more than 10 metres. However, don't be lulled into a false sense of security here. Even the smallest of slabs has claimed human lives.

### Loose Snow Avalanches

Loose snow avalanches occur most often after a heavy snowfall. They start small and get bigger as they pick up additional snow when progressing down the mountain. The snow is not consolidated, and therefore loose snow avalanches are often called powder avalanches. They can reach speeds of 300 km/h and are incredibly destructive.

## CORNICE COLLAPSE AVALANCHES

Cornice collapses are also of significant concern. Since cornices are formed by wind, the slope a cornice falls onto when it gives way is almost always wind-loaded and very unstable.

## ICE AVALANCHES

Similar to cornice collapses, ice avalanches are caused by unstable blocks of ice, commonly known as seracs. Seracs are found at the very edge of an overhanging glacier. When the stresses of gravity become too large, huge, house-sized chunks of ice can break off the glacier and come crashing down on the terrain below. The serac fall off the southeast side of Snowdome on the Athabasca Glacier is a classic example. Massive blocks of ice regularly separate from Snowdome's glacier, threatening travellers below. One of two routes up the Athabasca Glacier forces mountaineers to travel directly under these seracs. Needless to say, the traverse below the Snowdome seracs is a rapid and perhaps anxious one for many.

## RECOGNIZING AVALANCHE TERRAIN

Gaining the ability to recognize avalanche terrain is the first step in the complex process everyone must go through to ensure safe travel in winter. With proper training, lots of reading and a diligent effort in the backcountry, the following skills can be learned and developed quickly.

## SLOPE ANGLE

The most important factor in determining whether terrain has the potential to produce an avalanche is slope angle: angles between 25° and 60° have that potential. Generally, angles of 35° to 40° produce the largest number of slab avalanches. Slopes of these angles deserve the most scrutiny and should be carefully studied and tested before traversing or ascending them (see the next section, Recognizing Avalanche Potential, on page 47).

Measuring the angle of a particular slope is best accomplished using an inclinometer. Use of this tool is especially important when you are first developing avalanche-recognition skills. Putting a specific number to your own observations will dramatically increase your ability to accurately determine a slope angle without an inclinometer.

Always be aware that in regards to "eyeing" the angle of a particular slope, human perception has limitations. Often what appears to be low-angled can be far steeper than estimated and vice versa; this is something to think about when heading to that 20° slope that is actually 38°.

## Slope Orientation

The leeward slope is the side of the mountain that is opposite to the direction from which the wind is blowing. As such, it is usually wind-loaded and very unstable. In the Canadian Rockies, the primary wind direction is from west to east and southwest to northeast. Therefore, slopes facing east or northeast are far more likely to be avalanche-prone than those facing west or southwest. Remember that this is just a generalization and by no means implies that all west- and southwest-facing slopes are safe. Serious, destructive avalanches occur on all slopes.

## Slope Shape

Three terms describe slope shape: convex, concave and planar (see diagram on next page).

| CONCAVE | CONVEX | PLANAR |

MOUNT JOFFRE DISPLAYS THE THREE TYPES OF SLOPES.
C=CONCAVE, V=CONVEX, P=PLANAR.

Avalanches can occur on all three types; however, convex slopes present the most serious risk for a slide. The shape of a convex slope puts a great deal of stress on the snow just below the bulge. Always be on the lookout for convex slopes and be ready to assess possible consequences if they release.

Concave slopes, because of their bowl-like shape, are capable of supporting the weight of the snow above them to a greater degree than convex or planar slopes. This rule only applies to a certain extent, however. When that weight becomes excessive, concave slopes will release just like convex ones do. The location from which an avalanche may start on a concave slope is difficult to determine.

The consistent angle of planar slopes means they can avalanche anywhere.

## ANCHORS

As the word implies, anchors help keep snow attached to the slope it's on, thus rendering the slope more stable than one without anchors. Anchors include trees, vegetation and rocks. Unfortunately, like many other aspects of avalanche physics, anchoring is a double-edged sword. The snowpack around anchors is obviously thinner and therefore weaker and prone to instability. In other words, avalanches can start around anchors.

Forested terrain on a slope is typically a good indicator that the slope is relatively safe. When a slope is abundantly covered in full-grown trees, you know there has usually been little to no avalanche activity on that slope for a number of years. Ascending through heavily treed terrain is always preferable to being out on open steep slopes.

## ELEVATION

The categories of terrain and their corresponding ratings on the avalanche bulletin provide pretty clear evidence that the higher you go the more avalanche risk there is. On rare occasions the ratings may be the same in each zone, but the overwhelming majority of days will see a more severe rating for terrain in the alpine than below it. Increased elevation means more snow and more wind to blow that snow around. As a general rule, as soon as you move above treeline and into the alpine, expect the avalanche risk to rise.

## ATES

The Avalanche Terrain Exposure Scale takes all of the above into account and then provides a rating for the terrain in question. This important resource is discussed in more detail in the Ratings section on pages 36 and 37.

## RECOGNIZING AVALANCHE POTENTIAL

Recognizing avalanche terrain is the first step in the often complicated process of assessing snow stability. The next step is determining if that terrain has the potential to avalanche in its present condition. A leeward, 38°, convex slope is a recipe for disaster, but that doesn't mean it will slide. Are there weak and strong layers in the snowpack? Have recent changes in temperature or wind velocity affected the snowpack? When was the last major snowfall? Has the area been noted for persistent weak layers? These are just a few of many questions that have to be answered in order to determine avalanche potential.

### THE SNOWPACK

Entire books have been written about the complexities of the average snowpack and correct analysis of its slide potential. I will limit my discussion to a few rudimentary principles. Pick up one of the aforementioned books to read more about this interesting subject. Tony Daffern's *Avalanche Safety* is particularly good.

Over the course of the winter, the snowpack builds up in layers whose characteristics depend on the individual events of precipitation and wind. Temperature changes then transform the snowpack, creating areas of strong, well-bonded snow and areas of weak, cohesionless snow. Well-bonded snow is not necessarily a good thing. If it sits atop a weak layer, you have the makings of a slab avalanche: the weak layer may collapse during or after a major snowfall, causing the slab above to slide down the slope.

More important than the strength of a particular layer is the relative strength between layers. Snow layers sometimes bond together well and at other times do not. A weak bond between layers is a major cause of avalanches.

There are several ways in which you can test for and recognize layers in a snowpack, including the following.

### Pole Test

The pole test is fast and should be done frequently throughout any trip. It is good for determining where weak and strong layers are, as well as their corresponding thicknesses, but it will give you little information about how well these layers are bonded together. Gently push either the end of a basketless hiking pole or the handle end of a ski pole into the snow, perpendicular to the surface. Where layers of different strengths lie, you will feel different levels of resistance as you push. Pay special attention for strong layers lying atop weak layers.

### Snowpit Test

Digging a snowpit is far more time-consuming than conducting a pole test. However, a well-dug pit can be considerably more informative than a pole test, too. Pick an area in a safe location that is representative of the terrain you will be travelling on. Dig a pit approximately 1.5 metres deep and 1.5 metres wide, making the uphill wall and at least one side wall smooth and vertical. Even when digging the hole, your shovel will allow you to feel strong and weak layers, in much the same way a pole test does. It is also important to not disturb the snow on the uphill side of the pit, as this will obviously compress layers, rendering an analysis of the snowpack inaccurate.

Once the pit has been dug, brush away the light layer of excess snow from the walls to expose the snow layers. Layers or ridges that stand out from the wall indicate hard or strong layers, while weak layers will be indented into the wall. Again, look for strong layers atop weak layers. An especially lethal pattern to look for is (from bottom to top) hard layer, weak layer, strong layer (slab). If the weak layer collapses, the slab will fall onto the hard layer, which acts as a shear surface on which the slab can slide. Using a thin straightedge, such as a credit card, to run down and through the wall can help in feeling the layers. Pushing your fingers, fist or hard objects into the snow wall also helps you to determine the hardness of each layer.

While a pole test and a snowpit test both help you determine where the layers are and their relative hardness, they will not tell you anything about how well the layers are bonded together. For that purpose, you will have to conduct a shovel shear test, a compression test or a Rutschblock test.

### Shovel Shear Test

Dig a snowpit as previously described. Isolate a column of undisturbed snow about 30 centimetres deep and wide. Use a saw or string to cut downward through the back of the column. Insert the shovel at the back of the column and gently pull forward, noting if and where the column shears off along a clean plane. The easier it shears, the more unstable the snowpack is at the level of the shear. You can then apply a rating of Very Easy, Easy, Moderate, Hard or Very Hard, according to how much force was required to cause the shear. In general, Very Easy and Easy indicate unstable snow, whereas a rating of Moderate, Hard or Very Hard indicates a more stable snowpack of varying degrees. For more reliable results it is necessary to repeat the procedure at least once.

### Compression Test

A compression test is similar to a shovel shear test, except, instead of placing the shovel in the cut at the back, you place the shovel flat on top of the column. Gently tap the blade of the shovel and observe where the snow fails. Increase the strength of the taps as required. Again, the strength of the bond between layers is determined by the force (strength and number of taps) required to cause a failure. If no failure occurs, the snowpack may be quite stable.

### Rutschblock Test

Finally, the Rutschblock test (*ein Rutsch* is German for "a slide") determines how the snowpack responds to a person's weight and therefore is generally accepted as the most reliable test for characterizing the strength of the bond between layers. It is really a combination of a shovel shear and compression test, but on a much larger scale.

On a slope of at least 25°, but in a safe location, isolate a block of snow about 1.5 metres in all three dimensions (length, width, depth). Make a cut through the back of the block with a saw or string. Stand above the block, parallel to the cut on the back, with your snowshoes on, and then jump down onto the block, noting if and where a shear occurs. If no shear occurs, repeatedly jump on the block, increasing the force to try to make a failure. Ratings similar to those of the shovel shear and compression tests can then be applied to determine the strength between the layers.

## OTHER CLUES TO SNOWPACK INSTABILITY

Digging pits and performing shovel tests and any of the other tests mentioned above allow you to gather the information you need to help determine the strength of the snowpack, but they are not the only methods. There are audio, visual and weather-related clues to snowpack quality that also deserve a great deal of your attention.

### Whumphing

Whumphing is one of the most obvious and often frightening indicators of a weak snowpack that is just waiting to release.

Whumphing can be heard and/or felt. It is the very distinctive sound that accompanies the collapse of a layer of a small or large area of snow. It indicates an extreme instability in the snowpack. When whumphing occurs on a slope less steep than the required angle for a slide, there is little to be concerned about. Of course, this indicates that the snowpack is very unstable and tells you to stay away from terrain in the danger zone. If you hear a whumph on a slope that is between 25° and 60°, however, you should get off the slope immediately. You are already in a very precarious and dangerous area at this point. Turn around and follow your tracks out to safety.

### Visual clues

Fracture lines, evidence of wind loading and avalanche debris from previous activity all indicate a potentially dangerous area.

### Weather

Precipitation, wind and temperature can significantly affect the stability of the snowpack. Most natural avalanches occur during or immediately after an event of precipitation. This is because the event adds new weight and therefore new stress to the snowpack. Rain is particularly bad for weakening the snowpack. Snow in certain situations can actually strengthen the bonds between grains and between layers. However, this is not the general rule. Snowshoeing in avalanche terrain during or after a heavy snowfall is a very bad idea.

Wind also adds new weight to the snowpack by redistributing snow. In essence, a strong wind event is as effective as a heavy snowfall and may yield the same serious consequences. The direction of the wind is particularly important. A west wind blowing over a ridge that's oriented in a north–south direction may create unstable conditions on the east side of the ridge. Any slope that accumulates snow during a wind event is called a leeward slope. Leeward slopes are notorious for being unstable. The above scenario is very typical of the Canadian Rockies, where the winds are predominantly west and southwest. Avalanche bulletins in this part of the world are often littered with phrases like "stay away from east- and northeast-facing slopes." Also be aware of slopes that are side-loaded. This often occurs on slopes that have gullies or ribs running down. The leeward sides of the gullies can be very unstable.

While gradual temperature changes, specifically warming, may strengthen the snowpack, more dramatic swings in temperature can cause instability. Spring avalanches are commonly the result of the large temperature difference between morning and afternoon. For this reason it is wise to leave early and be off the mountain, or at least far away from avalanche terrain, before noon – either that or pick a long trip that has you descending very late in the day, after the temperature drops in the evening and the snowpack has had time to stabilize.

Even if the air temperature doesn't rise significantly during the day, direct sun (solar radiation) can warm the snowpack enough to cause avalanches. Blue sky may be great for the scenery, but it can also be responsible for dramatic increases in avalanche activity. The buildup of afternoon (sun-blocking) clouds may actually be a blessing.

### Attitude

It is quite surprising how important the role of attitude is in regards to risk assessment and backcountry safety. The process of gathering information about avalanche potential and then making an informed decision about whether or not to proceed would appear to be relatively straightforward. However, ambition, ego, pride, peer pressure or complacency can cloud your judgment in ways you may not think possible. Everyone with a decent background in avalanche awareness would know that a 35°, recently wind-loaded slope, with a persistent weak layer and noticeable fracture lines, is a recipe for disaster and claim they would stay well away from it. Unfortunately, the number of incidents on just such terrain indicates that people are sometimes ignoring the warning signs and proceeding anyway. I'm sure that almost every experienced backcountry enthusiast is guilty of poor judgment at least once in their travels. Don't let any of the above factors push you onto terrain that you shouldn't be putting to the test. The old cliché "the mountain is not going anywhere" is always fitting in such cases.

### Avoiding avalanches

While the process of gathering information may be straightforward, compiling data into something that promotes good decision-making in the mountains is complex and far from cut and dried. A 35° slope will not necessarily avalanche if the weather factors and snowpack criteria are favourable. However, if this is a leeward slope that has been recently wind-loaded, it now becomes very dangerous, even if the other criteria are still favourable. While recent avalanche activity is the most telling sign of dangerous terrain, if you approach a very dangerous slope early in the season that simply hasn't avalanched yet, you may be lulled into a false sense of security. These are just a couple of examples of how putting everything together and then making a decision is not always easy.

Avoiding avalanches begins with a thorough analysis of:

1. Terrain: slope angle and orientation;
2. Snowpack: slab formation, bonding between layers and sensitivity to weight; and
3. Weather: precipitation, wind and temperature.

When accurate information regarding these elements has been gathered, it becomes easier to piece the puzzle together into a coherent analysis and then proceed accordingly.

## AVALANCHE GEAR

There are three components of avalanche gear: a transceiver, a probe and a shovel. Learning to use them properly is best done by taking an avalanche awareness course and then practising in a safe location.

Transceivers, commonly referred to as beacons, send and receive a radio signal that is used to locate buried victims of avalanches. Beacons can be analog or digital. Analog beacons emit an audible tone that gets louder when the receiving beacons gets close to the transmitting beacon. Digital beacons use an arrow to point the locator in the right direction. It may sound as though beacons are very easy to use. Everyone who has tried to locate another beacon with their own knows this is not the case. Again, take a course to learn about the intricacies of beacon use.

Probes are typically 2.5–3.0 metres long and retract to about 0.5 m. They are used to find the specific location of a buried person after the beacon has ascertained the general location. Simply push the probe into the snow until it makes contact with the buried person.

An avalanche shovel is absolutely mandatory when travelling in avalanche country. Trying to dig out a buried person without one is next to impossible. Typically the snow sets like concrete around an avalanche victim, making it exceedingly difficult to use your hands as shovels. An avalanche shovel is also essential for digging pits and performing shovel shear tests.

## AVALANCHE RESCUE

Again, this topic needs to be covered by a professional in classroom and field settings. However, the following basic points are offered here.

If you get caught in an avalanche:

1. Shout and make noise to help others locate you.
2. If your pack is heavy, try to take it off, as it may drag you down under the snow. The flipside is that a pack may also protect you from injury.
3. Unfortunately, it is highly unlikely you will have time to remove your snowshoes. They may do major damage to your legs as the snow tosses you around. Snowshoes may also drag you down below the snow surface.
4. Try to stay on the surface of the snow by using swimming motions.
5. When the snow begins to stop, try to create an air pocket to breathe by cupping your hand over your mouth.

If you see someone caught in an avalanche:

1. Watch them very carefully as they go down. If they disappear under the snow, watch the motion of the mass of snow where they disappeared. Do not start running toward their position until the slide has stopped.
2. When the slide has stopped, look around for other potential slides and hazards before you initiate a rescue.
3. If you are in a party with several people, make a plan of action and delegate tasks and specific areas for each person.
4. Do not send a party member to get help. All persons should engage in the rescue attempt.
5. Immediately have everyone turn their beacon to Receive mode.
6. Mark the spot where the victim was last seen. Search downslope from this spot.
7. Look for clues such as clothing and equipment to help narrow down the location.
8. When you locate the victim, starting digging but try not to trample the snow down, as it may compromise the victim's airspace.

9. Try to uncover the victim's head and chest first. Then remove the snow around the entire body. Be aware that they may have serious injuries and that moving them may aggravate those injuries.

10. Once the victim is located and dug out, send someone to get help immediately. If possible, call 911 as soon as you are able.

## IN CONCLUSION

Perhaps the most sobering fact in everyone's quest to avoid avalanches is that you can do everything right and still get caught in a slide. Even with today's greater understanding of the physics of snow and avalanche causes, avalanches can still be highly unpredictable. If all this "scary" reading is of great concern to you, it may be better to stick to routes with no or low avalanche danger. The wonderful aspect of the Canadian Rockies is that you could probably spend a lifetime exploring the amazing terrain and never need to cross, ascend or get anywhere near an avalanche slope.

On the other side of the coin, try not to let fear paralyze you and keep you from enjoying some of the best scenery on the planet. Approach the situation simply: educate yourself; seek education from professionals; talk to others who have experience; start off on easy low hazard trips and work your way up; go on trips with people who have experience and can share their knowledge with you; and always remember that playing it safe means you'll live to try again when conditions are better.

## OTHER HAZARDS AND CONSIDERATIONS

While of primary concern, avalanches are certainly not the only elements of nature to be cognizant of. Cornices, glaciers and bad weather can be just as deadly.

## CORNICES

Cornices are one of my favourite aspects of winter travel. These shapely and unique formations can add tremendously to the scenery and views on any trip. However, they can also be a source of great danger. Having a cornice collapse beneath you will probably have deadly consequences. As it may be difficult to ascertain whether there is solid rock beneath the snow you are travelling on, it is always best to play it safe by staying far away from the edge when snowshoeing or hiking along a ridge. You can use a trekking pole, a ski pole or an avalanche probe to determine if solid ground is underfoot, but you need to be careful in discerning whether your pole is striking solid ground or just a hard layer of snow or ice. Cornices can grow to enormous sizes and may overhang the edge of a ridge by a significant distance.

THE LARGE CORNICE ON THE SUMMIT RIDGE OF MOUNT NESTOR.

ABOVE: A LARGE OVERHANGING CORNICE ON KENT RIDGE NORTH.
BELOW: MARK PASSES A LARGE CREVASSE ON GLACIER DES POILUS.
IN WINTER THIS CREVASSE WOULD BE COVERED BY A SNOWBRIDGE,
TURNING IT INTO A POSSIBLE DEATH TRAP.

## Glaciers and Crevasses

Hopefully, it goes without saying that anyone stepping onto a glacier should have taken a course in glacier travel and crevasse rescue. (See Snowshoe Mountaineering on page 20.)

## Bad Weather

Inclement weather can be troublesome at any time of the year, but the trouble it causes is especially pronounced in the winter months. Getting caught in a snowstorm with whiteout conditions can be very serious. A storm will quickly cover up the tracks you made, making it difficult to retrace your steps. Using a GPS unit, wands or flags to mark your route is strongly advised when bad weather is a possibility. Better yet, refer to the section below entitled Picking Good Weather Days (page 60), and try to avoid nasty weather completely. If you do choose to go out when the weather is suspect, pick easy routes with few or no hazards and straightforward routefinding.

## Limited Daylight

On December 21 of each year, the mountain parks receive a little less than eight hours of daylight. That's not a large number when compared to the 16.5 hours we get on June 21. Plan your day accordingly and always have a headlamp with extra batteries in your backpack. A forced bivouac in winter is not only unsavoury because of the cold temperatures but also because you may have as much as 16 hours of darkness to get through.

Mountain Standard Time (November–March) also means that early starts are almost imperative. Thankfully, the situation dramatically improves after the second Sunday in March, when the clocks move ahead an hour. This doesn't impact the amount of daylight hours but at least puts the sunset an hour later, allowing for longer trips or later starts.

# PICKING GOOD WEATHER DAYS

Snowshoeing is very much a good-weather activity. Lacking the exhilarating run down that skiers are accustomed to, or the speed of a snowmobile, the primary thrill of snowshoeing comes from experiencing the beautiful surroundings. Clear skies enhance that experience to an infinite degree.

Predicting the weather in the Canadian Rockies is often a crapshoot at best. Many meteorological factors contribute to the uncertainty of weather forecasting here, factors that render even the most experienced and knowledgeable forecasters incapable of accurate prediction of the weather. In short, be prepared for any type of weather and be understanding when the weather is not as glorious as one of the local forecasters predicted. Of course, many times I've gone to the mountains, a bad weather forecast in hand, only to enjoy beautifully clear skies.

Here are some procedures to go through and some tips for maximizing the amount of time you spend under clear skies and minimizing that spent under cloudy skies.

1. Check the weather forecasts online. Environment Canada and The Weather Network are presently the most popular online sources for weather in Canada. Monitor the forecasts several days before your trip, but expect them to change frequently. Always check again the night before your trip and if possible the morning of the trip.

2. Look at a current satellite image just before the trip. Sometimes the satellite image very much contradicts the forecast. In general, I trust a satellite image far more than a computer-generated forecast. Knowing how to read and analyze weather patterns from satellite images can be a very useful skill and may save you from spending a frustrating day in bad weather.

3. High-pressure systems are your best friend. When the forecaster on the local news mentions "a ridge of high pressure," start salivating and do your best to get out to the mountains. High-pressure systems are generally predictable and stable and result in the best possible weather.

4. Be flexible in regards to changing your plans at the last minute. Bad weather in one area of the Rockies does not mean bad weather throughout. In general, the farther west and the farther north you go, the worse the weather. The Front Ranges may be basking in full sunshine while mountains of the Continental Divide are covered over with clouds.

As stated in the avalanche section, the downside to clear, sunny skies is that they can have an enormously detrimental effect on the snowpack; the sun can weaken bonds between layers very quickly. This is pronounced on south-, southwest- and west-facing slopes that receive the brunt of the sun's rays as the day goes on. Getting a very early start and staying off avalanche-prone slopes later in the day is the solution to this problem. It may also become necessary to wait until much later in the day to descend if snow conditions deteriorate. The cooler temperatures of evening will hopefully strengthen the snowpack again. If not, you may be looking at a forced bivy and/or a helicopter rescue.

THE DEEP-BLUE SKY THAT OFTEN ACCOMPANIES A HIGH-PRESSURE SYSTEM. OF COURSE THE SUN MUST BE IN THE RIGHT POSITION.

All of the above doesn't mean you should stay at home on cloudy days. Sometimes cloud cover can lead to very atmospheric lighting and views. Also, on very rare occasions, the clouds may be lying very low in the valley, allowing you to ascend above them. This always provides an unbeatable experience.

## SNOWSHOEING TECHNIQUE

You would think snowshoeing requires little, if any, technique. After all, it's simply walking with short "planks" on your feet. Certainly snowshoeing does not require all the skill and technique that accomplished backcountry skiers possess, but there still exist general snowshoe techniques that will make snowshoeing an efficient, safe and enjoyable experience.

BELOW: ON AN ASCENT OF WHIRLPOOL RIDGE,
LOW-LYING CLOUDS BLANKET THE VALLEY BELOW.
OPPOSITE: A SHAPELY CORNICE AND LOW-LYING
CLOUDS ON AN ASCENT OF KENT RIDGE OUTLIER.

## GETTING UP

Snowshoeing on flat and gentle terrain is no different than simple walking. However, for steeper terrain, here are some different techniques you may wish to employ and useful tips to keep in mind.

1. If your snowshoes have them, put up the heel lifts to reduce strain on your calf muscles and Achilles tendon.
2. Snowshoe in switchback patterns so that you are not going directly up a steep slope.
3. If the snow on steeper slopes is soft, kick-step into it with your snowshoes, then flatten the snow by stepping down into it.
4. If the snow is hard, you will want snowshoes with crampons. The best styles are advanced models that provide for the frame of the snowshoe to act as a crampon. When using this type of snowshoe, maximize the amount of the frame

*LEFT: GOING STRAIGHT UP RELATIVELY GENTLE SLOPES ON MOUNT RHONDDA. RIGHT: USING A HERRINGBONE TECHNIQUE ON THE SAME SLOPE HIGHER UP.*

making contact with the hard snow surface. Frame-crampon snowshoes can tackle slopes up to a very steep 35°.

5. For steeper slopes of soft snow, a similar technique to the skiing herringbone (feet angled out) may work better than switchbacking (see photos).

## GETTING DOWN

Like ascending, descending gentle slopes on snowshoes is very easy. Plunge-stepping and even running downhill can be fun and will get you down in no time at all. Steeper slopes require more attention to technique. When going downhill, keep the following tips in mind:

1. Bend your knees slightly and keep your weight over your feet. Avoid the temptation to lean forward. Use poles for balance and support.

DESCENDING A STEEP SLOPE BY FACING IN AND KICK-STEPPING.

2. For steeper slopes, it may be necessary to face into the slope and descend using a kick-stepping technique. Your poles can be used for balance and also in a self-belay technique, similar to that used with an ice axe.

## SIDE-SLOPING

When side-sloping (traversing) go slightly uphill as you go across.

1. In soft snow, kick-step into the slope with the inside edge of your snowshoe.
2. In hard snow, use the snowshoes' crampons. Traversing very steep slopes may require you to face into the slope and move sideways, keeping your snowshoes pointed uphill. This technique allows for the most effective use of the snowshoes' crampons.

*TRAVERSING A STEEP SLOPE OF HARD SNOW —*
*HEEL LIFTS UP, SNOWSHOES POINTING FORWARD.*

## Glissading and Crazy Carpets

Glissading is the act of sliding down a snow slope on your butt. It can be a fun and extremely effective way of travelling down a hill, but it also often requires some technical skill. Depending on the angle of the slope and the conditions of the snow, you will most likely need an ice axe. Practise using an axe to control your speed, and self-arrest on low-angled slopes with long and safe runouts. Again, the Snow and Ice Long Weekend course is an excellent place to learn the proper techniques of glissading, from a professional. **Never glissade wearing snowshoes or foot crampons**.

One of the most enjoyable ways to get down a snow slope involves using a Crazy Carpet. The whole concept may sound a little childish, but if it works and it's also fun, why the heck not! Crazy Carpets are very inexpensive, extremely light and easy to use.

There are two ways to ride a Crazy Carpet: sitting down or lying on your stomach. The sitting position is the most popular, especially for steeper slopes. Remember to take your snowshoes off if sitting, and never wear crampons. The seated position gives you a great deal of control over the carpet. It's also very easy to roll off the carpet if your speed becomes too great (a much harder manoeuvre if you are lying on your stomach). Consider how you are going to place your legs and feet before you start out. For the steepest slopes, and the most control, place both legs off the carpet and use your feet like brakes to control your speed. If you want to go faster, sit cross-legged with one or both legs on the carpet.

The only problem you are likely to encounter is how to sit on the carpet with a backpack that probably has your snowshoes fastened to it. Position the shoes high on the sides of your pack or on top to prevent them from dragging on the snow.

Although I have not had the opportunity to do so, I'm told that lying on your stomach and using your snowshoes as brakes and rudders is also very effective and fun. I would be very cautious about using this method on steeper slopes.

Note that using a Crazy Carpet will, for the most part, not save you a great amount of time, if any. The process of changing back and forth from snowshoes to Crazy Carpet is time-consuming. Unless you are carpeting down a significantly long slope, the quick-descent benefits will be negated by the time you spend changing back and forth. Most will use a Crazy Carpet simply for the sheer thrill and enjoyment of it.

## SNOWSHOEING ETIQUETTE

As more and more people make their way into the mountains on snowshoes, the use of good etiquette becomes increasingly important. There really isn't much to snowshoe etiquette, but in following and respecting a few basic guidelines we can ensure a good relationship with all mountain users, such as skiers, hikers and snowmobilers.

### SKI TRACKS AND TRAIL-BREAKING

The most important guideline for snowshoers is to avoid snowshoeing on ski tracks whenever possible. Many winter trails are wide enough to support separate trails for skiers and snowshoers. If a ski trail has already been established on the route you are on, make a new trail for snowshoers as far away as from the ski trail as possible. This may seem like a great deal of effort when an established trail is right there, but trail-breaking is the price of travel for all winter users. At some point, everyone must take on the burden of breaking new trail. If all travellers share that responsibility, then it is possible you may only have to break new trail a few times each season. Everyone who follows on the new trail will appreciate your efforts, and skiers will also be thankful you have stayed off an established ski trail.

For trails with no visible signs of snowshoe tracks, try to stay to the far right on the way in and the same side on the way back out. The right side is an arbitrary choice on my part; however, it is probable that skiers will use the right side on the way in, when they are moving at the slower speed, and the left on the way out, when they are moving much faster. Using one side for both directions of snowshoe travel may help to eliminate collisions. If snowshoers get into the habit of using the right side going in, a rule of etiquette may develop over time. This will invariably make life easier for all winter travellers and minimize conflict. Note that snowshoers should always use the same track going in and out, whereas skiers may choose to make a separate trail for their return trip to avoid skiing into one another.

The following heavy-traffic trails or routes described in this book are all wide enough to accommodate both ski and snowshoe trails, though there may be some sections where users must share the trail:

1. Burstall Pass (see page 202)
2. French Creek (see page 210)
3. Approach to the Bow Hut (see page 321)
4. Middle Kootenay Pass (see page 102)
5. Pocaterra Cirque (see page 139)

Trails or routes that are not wide enough to support both a ski trail and a snowshoe trail present a problem. Unfortunately the solution is not a perfect one. The route to North Buller Pass is a prime example. This well-used established summer trail is also used frequently in winter. The trail is narrow and heavily treed on both sides. Creating two trails is not a possibility. In this case, and some others, winter travellers must concede that the trail will be shared and be considerate of one another. Snowshoers should do their best to minimize damage to any existing ski trail, and skiers must acknowledge the right of snowshoers to be there and be open to the idea that a snowshoer or hiker may have broken the trail initially. The following trails have sections where snowshoers and skiers will probably have to share the same trail:

1. North Buller Pass (see page 158)
2. Smuts Pass (see page 175)
3. "Commonwealth Ridge" (see page 186)
4. Rummel Lake (see page 163)

Regarding trail-breaking on any trail – narrow or accommodating – a point of contention may arise after a heavy snowfall has sufficiently covered an established trail. In this situation the responsibility of trail-breaking falls upon the first party to start along the trail. If at all possible, snowshoers should try to avoid breaking trail over what may have been a ski track before the new snow arrived. Again, staying well over to the right side may be the best solution.

Simple common courtesy and decency, however, should be enough to avert any conflict between the different types of winter travellers. Remember, we all share a common goal – to enjoy the beauty of the mountains.

## Official Ski Trails

Groomed trails specifically for cross-country skiers are a little different from unofficial ski trails, such as the one to Burstall Pass. Snowshoers should try to avoid groomed trails completely. Damage to these trails, especially early in the season, can be dangerous to skiers, who might ski into a hole made by snowshoers or hikers. Serious injury can result from such a ski accidents. Later in the season, these trails are usually well packed down and less susceptible to serious damage, but snowshoers should still stay away from them.

There are exceptions to this general rule. Some groomed trails provide the only access into certain areas. Where this is the case, it may be necessary for snowshoers to use the trails, but they should always minimize the amount of time spent on them. Fortunately, for the most part, these trails are very wide, and getting in the way of skiers shouldn't be an issue. The trails leading out from the Shark Mountain (see page 169) parking lot are good examples.

Avoid the following areas if possible:

1. Elk Pass (except the official snowshoe trail) (see page 337)
2. Pocaterra, off Kananaskis Trail (see page 139)
3. Shark; use only to access the south end of Spray Lake and Mount Fortune (see page 169)

There are plenty of places to snowshoe in the Rockies without resorting to groomed trails. Be considerate and stay away from them.

## Official Snowshoe Trails

At present there are many unofficial snowshoe trails but very few official ones. The provincial and national parks have made an excellent effort to increase the number of official snowshoe trails and will probably continue to do so. Official trails are a great place to start for beginners. They are usually relatively flat and short and have few to no objective hazards. Refer to Appendix D (see page 337) for a list of official snowshoe trails in Kananaskis.

## Right of Way

This point of etiquette is a simple one to practise and far less potentially contentious than the trail-breaking issue. Very simply, parties that travel faster have the right of way. For example, skiers are faster than snowshoers. Even on level or uphill terrain, skiers move at a slightly faster speed. Always be aware of this and move over to the right side of the trail to let skiers pass if required. Hopefully you'll be on different trails so moving over won't be necessary.

Obviously, the difference in speed between skiers and snowshoers is far more pronounced when going downhill. Try to stay to the correct side of the trail and make yourself visible to skiers when going down through treed terrain. Wearing bright-coloured clothing is always a good idea. When in treed terrain, moving completely off the trail to let skiers pass is the best course of action.

### Snowmobilers and snowmobile trails

The etiquette of right of way applies doubly when you encounter snowmobilers. Not only should you move over for them but you should also get completely off the trail when they approach and pass. If this happens to put you in a metre and a half of snow, so be it! Snowmobilers can move at terrific speeds. Being struck by a fast-moving, 80-kilogram skier would be very unpleasant; being struck by that same 80-kilogram person atop a 260-kilogram snowmobile, both moving at 60 km/h, would ruin your day in a big way! Snowmobiles are very noisy and so you will be afforded plenty of warning that one is coming your way. Try to make yourself visible to snowmobilers, even when you are well off the trail.

Snowmobiling is not permitted in Banff and Jasper national parks, nor is it allowed in most of the Kananaskis region. Therefore you are only likely to encounter snowmobilers in areas such as the following:

1. Castle Crown (see page 100)
2. Parts of South Kananaskis (Highway 940 south) (see page 117)
3. Around Bragg Creek (McLean Creek)

Note that snowshoeing on snowmobile tracks is an accepted practice, unlike snowshoeing on ski tracks.

## Conclusion

Hopefully the preceding text has not only been informative but has also served to pique your interest in the exciting sport of snowshoeing and related winter activities in the mountains. As discussed, snowshoeing can be as simple or as complex as you want it to be. However, regardless of the level of trip you are undertaking, it is extremely important to be informed about the dangers of the environment you will be in; etiquette in that environment; choosing appropriate objectives for the conditions and for your skill level; and taking the appropriate gear. The Canadian Rockies is an inherently dangerous environment, but snowshoeing in the Rockies does not have to be a dangerous activity. Be informed, be aware of your strengths and limitations, be sensible, know what you are getting into, and always err on the side of caution.

Now on to the good stuff: the trips!

# THE TRIPS

The routes in this book cover many areas of the southern Canadian Rockies, from majestic Waterton in the far south to the spectacular Columbia Icefield, about 600 kilometres to the northwest. The lack of routes for some areas does not mean they are not snowshoe friendly – it simply means I have yet to explore those areas fully. The Kananaskis area is heavily favoured, simply because snowshoe routes in Kananaskis are easy to get to and there are plenty of them. The snow, especially in the west section of Kananaskis, comes early and stays late. Kananaskis is also the only area in the Canadian Rockies where official snowshoe trails have been designated.

Each area detailed in the following pages offers opportunities for easy snowshoe trips and serious snowshoe mountaineering trips. Needless to say, the scenery and views throughout the Rockies are fantastic, regardless of the area you choose to snowshoe in. Personally, my favourite destinations are Waterton, Highway 742 in Kananaskis, and the valley north of Mount Saskatchewan. The latter and Waterton will definitely provide a measure of seclusion, if that is what you are looking for.

Two final reminders before you set out: read the introductory information for each trip carefully so that you are aware of the level of the trip, gear requirements and objective hazards; and check the avalanche bulletin and the weather forecast before you set out.

You are now ready to explore one of the most magical environments this planet has to offer – enjoy!

# WATERTON

*The amenities at Waterton Lakes National Park basically close down during the winter and much of spring. Services are minimal at this time of year, and the only road that continues to give access to the mountains is the Akamina Parkway. Nevertheless, there are several extremely enjoyable snowshoe routes in this park if you happen to be in the area.*

*On average, Waterton receives almost six metres of snow per year. Much of that snow is displaced by the intense winds common to the area. Thus, west-facing slopes can often be blown free of snow, while lee areas accumulate enormous deposits of snow. Be aware of this as you choose routes.*

*It is also wise to keep in mind that the vicious Waterton winds can cause tremendous disparities in temperature from ground level to mountaintop. I distinctly remember a forecast high temperature of +12 °C for the Waterton townsite when we completed the Mount Lineham trip in April 2010. With the wind-chill factor, the temperature on the summit was approximately −25 °C; that's a difference of a whopping 37°C! Two days after our Lineham trip, we encountered wind chills that were around −40 °C at the Carthew–Alderson col, due to an 80+ km/h wind. These two examples should illustrate that you must be prepared for bone-chilling temperatures regardless of the forecast high, and avoid summits and exposed areas when the wind is predicted to be strong.*

*Also bear in mind that weather forecasts for Waterton Lakes*

National Park centre on the townsite. Given its close proximity to the Continental Divide (a magnet for bad weather), it is not unusual for the town to be basking in full sun while all "you know what" is breaking loose only several kilometres west.

With the exception of Forum Ridge, all routes in this area require avalanche gear.

BEAUTIFUL WINTER SCENERY ON FORUM PEAK, WATERTON LAKES NATIONAL PARK.

# 1 RUBY RIDGE

(MAP 1, PAGE 312)

| | |
|---|---|
| DIFFICULTY | MODERATE |
| HAZARD | HIGH; ATES 3 |
| MOUNTAIN HEIGHT | 2430 M |
| ELEVATION GAIN | 870 M |
| ROUND-TRIP DISTANCE | 6 KM |
| ROUND-TRIP TIME | 5–7 HOURS |
| ADDITIONAL EQUIPMENT | AVALANCHE GEAR |
| MAPS | 82 G/1 SAGE CREEK, 82 H/4 WATERTON LAKES, GEM TREK WATERTON LAKES NATIONAL PARK |

*Ruby Ridge has grand views of some of the more statuesque peaks in Waterton Park. While the ascent is relatively straightforward, getting to the ascent slope does involve traversing avalanche slopes. The upper slopes are often windblown clear of snow. If so, expect to finish the ascent on foot.*

## DIRECTIONS

Drive 9.3 km on Cameron Lake Road and park at the pull-out on the right (north) side of the road. This is the Lineham Creek trailhead. Note that the trailhead sign is sometimes removed during the winter months.

If the Lineham Creek trail has been broken it is very easy to follow. If not, don't fret; just follow the clear path through the trees in a WNW direction. In general, the trail parallels Lineham Creek (at a distance) for a while, makes a couple of short switchbacks to higher terrain, and shortly after breaks out into the open. When the terrain opens up, it is time to make one of two route decisions.

*Snow-free route*

If the slopes in front of you are snow-free, it is possible to ascend practically anywhere. Leave the trail and travel upslope, going due north and following the line of least resistance. Expect to encounter several false summits before reaching the true one. Routefinding is easy as long as you are going up. Take some time to enjoy the beautiful outcrops of red and green argillite and other colourful varieties of rock if they are visible.

*Snow-covered route*

More than likely, the lower slopes will not be snow-free, and the following route is suggested. When the terrain opens up keep following the trail as it side-slopes the south side of Ruby (**avalanche danger here**). Remember that you may be the first travellers of the season and will have to break new trail – stay just above the trees. Some of the slopes here are quite steep and will avalanche under the right conditions. Also be aware that the slopes above and to the right could release. An aggressive set of crampons on your snowshoes may be required if the snow on the wind-ravaged slopes is hard.

Side-slope around the southwest side of the mountain for about 1 km (**avalanche danger throughout this traverse**) before arriving at the thick line of trees ascending NE up Ruby Ridge. This line of trees provides the safest route to the gentler terrain of the upper slopes. Upon reaching the trees, take a hard right and ascend through the trees to the upper slopes. Above treeline, continue going NE to the summit at GR182408. As in the snow-free route above, expect several false summits and a little more plodding than you might think.

At the summit, if the view of Waterton's highest peak, Mount Blakiston, does not satiate, I'm sure the vistas including

Cameron Lake and the peaks to the south, in Glacier National Park, will. Continuing east to the slightly lower summit is not recommended unless the slopes are snow-free. There are many small rock-bands in that area that must be downclimbed or circumvented. When snow-covered these rock-bands can be very dangerous. Instead, return the same way you came in. Unless you are positive the south slopes are snow-free, avoid trying to blaze a shortcut down the mountain by going directly south to the Lineham Creek trail.

A STUNNING SUNRISE BEFORE OUR ASCENT OF RUBY RIDGE. UNFORTUNATELY, THAT WAS THE BEST OF IT — THE WEATHER WAS TERRIBLE ALL DAY.

# 2 MOUNT LINEHAM

| | |
|---|---|
| **DIFFICULTY** DIFFICULT | |
| **HAZARD** HIGH | |
| **MOUNTAIN HEIGHT** 2730 M | |
| **ELEVATION GAIN** 1140 M | |
| **ROUND-TRIP DISTANCE** 10 KM | |
| **ROUND-TRIP TIME** 5.5–9 HOURS | |
| **ADDITIONAL EQUIPMENT** AVALANCHE GEAR, CRAMPONS (OPTIONAL), ICE AXE | |
| **MAPS** 82 G/1 SAGE CREEK, GEM TREK WATERTON LAKES NATIONAL PARK | |

*As one of the loftiest peaks in Waterton Park, Mount Lineham offers a phenomenal summit view. The south slopes also allow for one of the longest glissades of any of the peaks in this book. Take an ice axe (and perhaps a Crazy Carpet) if you want to experience the ride down. This trip favours very late-season attempts, when the snowpack is more stable and opportunities to avoid the snow altogether are more likely than they are earlier in the season. The route described here is very similar to that given in Alan Kane's* Scrambles in the Canadian Rockies *– just a few minor differences.*

## DIRECTIONS

Drive 10.5 km along Cameron Lake Road and park on the right side at the Rowe Lakes trailhead. From the parking lot, follow the Rowe Lakes trail to the south slopes of Mount Lineham. If the trail has already been broken, the trip will be an easy task. If not, try to follow the official trail as much as possible. It is obvious in most places, but not so much in others.

The trail parallels Rowe Creek for several hundred metres. When the first glimpse of Mount Lineham appears in front of you, the trail turns sharply to the right, gains some elevation and switches back to the left. It then resumes its westward direction, again paralleling Rowe Creek, but high above it now.

Eventually, you'll reach a more open area, with some impressive walls of rock and open slopes to the right. Traverse the open slopes, staying high, and find the trail on the other side (see photo A below). Continue going west for another 1–1.5 km, arriving at the base of a big avalanche slope around GR155380, 1921 m (see photo B opposite). If the trail has been broken all the way it should take about 1.5–2 hours to reach this point. Expect to take considerably longer if you have to break new trail all the way. For those using GPS technology, a waypoint here will be very useful if you choose to descend via an alternative route.

[A] *STAY HIGH AND FIND THE TRAIL ON THE OTHER SIDE.*

[B] THE BASE OF THE AVALANCHE SLOPE WHERE YOU
LEAVE THE TRAIL AND START UP MOUNT LINEHAM.
AV=AVALANCHE SLOPE. SR=SAFER ROUTE.

Turn right (north) and proceed up the right side of the avalanche slope. Obviously, the specific route you take will depend on avalanche conditions. Late in the season, when the snowpack is more stable than it was earlier, going directly up the avalanche slope is usually fine (**avalanche danger**). Nevertheless, it is better to hug the right side of the slope, just in case you need to escape to safer terrain in the trees. The slope veers to the right as it gains elevation, and your path should follow that trend. You probably will be salivating all the way up just thinking about the glissade potential on this slope!

If avalanche conditions are at all suspect, **do not** go up the avalanche slope. Instead, go to the right and ascend the south slopes of Lineham in the trees. You are not safe even on this route, however, because the trees eventually disappear and you will be subject to more **avalanche danger**, just higher up the slope. Err heavily on the side of caution throughout this trip. Visiting Lower Rowe Lake instead is always an acceptable consolation prize.

Regardless of the specific route you choose to take, routefinding is hardly an issue on this trip – go up; the summit is due north. Expect some slightly steeper terrain (35°) as you approach the summit. With a decent set of crampons on your snowshoes, you should be able to reach the summit with snowshoes on your feet. Otherwise, step-kick or use foot crampons for the upper slopes. The summit lies at GR156394, 2728 m. On a clear day, the summit view is unbeatable. Especially noteworthy is the horseshoe ridge of mounts Lineham, Hawkins and Blakiston, as well as their steep walls surrounding the Lineham Lakes far below. A host of shapely peaks to the south in Glacier National Park should also have your camera working overtime.

Time and energy permitting, extending the trip to hit two highpoints of the ridge west of Lineham provides a wonderfully scenic add-on to the day. If not, return the same way you came in. Most people will want to lose a couple of hundred metres of vertical elevation before they start the terrific glissade down. Again, using foot crampons instead of snowshoes when descending this first part before the glissade will allow for much better footing on the slope.

## EXTENSION TO GR133390

*The west ridge of Mount Lineham is magnificent: gentle slopes on the left and hair-raising drop-offs on the right, terrific rock colours (if they aren't snow-covered) and tons of gorgeous peaks to ogle along the way. Expect to add 200 vertical m, 4 horizontal km and about 3 hours for this extension.*

## DIRECTIONS

Travel is generally easy; just watch for huge cornices to your right. Two highpoints, the first at GR138392 and the second at GR133390, make terrific destinations (see photo C). The final few metres of the ascent slope to 133390 can be tricky, as the least steep route gets very close to the cornice overhanging the north side (**avalanche danger** and **free-fall danger**). Picking a line farther left puts you onto some serious avalanche terrain.

From 133390, it does appear to be possible to extend the trip even farther by heading north to two additional highpoints and then swinging around to the east to the summit of Mount Hawkins. I have not completed this extension on snowshoes, so I

[C] THE POSSIBLE EXTENSIONS OF MOUNT LINEHAM:
GR1 GR138392, GR2 GR133390.

can't say for sure it will go, but the summer route is simple ridge-walking. Completing this extension of an extension will require some serious stamina – there's a case of Moosehead beer waiting in my fridge for anyone who completes this possible extension and makes it out alive! For the rest of us mere mortals, GR133390 will, in spades, suffice.

To get back to the warmth of your vehicle there are two options.

### Glissade route

If you have your heart set on the amazing glissade down the south face of Lineham, return to the summit of Lineham (about 300 additional vertical m of elevation gain) and then follow the instructions described previously (see page 84).

### Walking descent route

To avoid the significant elevation gain of the glissade route, start by descending the way you came. Instead of regaining the high-point at GR138392, side-slope heading down and east (see photo D). This is the official trail, and late in the season it may be visible. Soon the trail curves back to the west and then south. You **do not** want to take this route, especially if large cornices are overhanging the ridge above. Continue going down and southeast into the treed terrain. When there, start going more down than southeast. There are unseen cliff-bands in front if you stay high too long. Descend into the valley and try to find the Rowe Lakes trail around GR145383. If you can't find it, simply head due east, back to where you left the main trail at the avalanche ascent slope. Once you are back at the main trail, the remainder of the descent will be mercifully easy and will only take about 45–55 minutes.

[D] LOOKING AT THE ALTERNATIVE DESCENT. THE ROUTE STAYS HIGH, TRAVERSING SLOPES INTO THE TREED TERRAIN AT THE LEFT MIDDLE OF THE PHOTO.

# 3 "CARTHEW MINOR"

(MAP 1, PAGE 312)

| | |
|---|---|
| **DIFFICULTY** EASY TO SUMMIT LAKE, DIFFICULT TO CARTHEW MINOR | |
| **HAZARD** MODERATE TO SUMMIT LAKE (ATES 2), HIGH TO CARTHEW MINOR | |
| **MOUNTAIN HEIGHT** SUMMIT LAKE 1920 M, CARTHEW MINOR 2327 M | |
| **ELEVATION GAIN** SUMMIT LAKE 300 M, CARTHEW MINOR 700 M | |
| **ROUND-TRIP DISTANCE** 13.6 KM TO SUMMIT LAKE, 16.4 KM TO CARTHEW MINOR | |
| **ROUND-TRIP TIME** 4.5–6 HOURS FOR SUMMIT LAKE, 5.5–7 HOURS FOR CARTHEW MINOR | |
| **ADDITIONAL EQUIPMENT** AVALANCHE GEAR, POSSIBLY CRAMPONS AND ICE AXE | |
| **MAPS** 82 G/1 SAGE CREEK, GEM TREK WATERTON LAKES NATIONAL PARK | |

*A trip to Summit Lake is a pleasant and generally easy outing. While views from the lake are quite respectable, the panorama from nearby "Carthew Minor" is spectacular. Unofficially named Carthew Minor is an outlier situated at the southwest end of Mount Carthew. The ascent of Carthew Minor is quite steep for several short sections. As well as stable snow conditions, snow-shoes with aggressive crampons and possibly frame crampons will be required to make this trip. You can also try the trip with foot crampons and an ice axe.*

## DIRECTIONS

Turn onto Cameron Lake Road and drive to the blockade at the end. Turn left into the parking area and find a place to park. Return to the road and hike or snowshoe about 2.5 km to Cameron Lake. The road is heavily used and well packed down. Hiking is usually faster than snowshoeing.

From the north end of Cameron Lake the summit of Carthew Minor is visible due east. Turn left (east) and follow the official summer trail near the shoreline. Much of this trail is wide enough for both ski and snowshoe tracks. Break a new snowshoe trail if necessary. The trail soon leaves the lake and starts uphill at a gentle grade. It then follows a series of long switchbacks up the hillside. If you are the first to break the snow trail, it may be hard to follow the exact summer route. As long as your general direction is east, you shouldn't have any problems.

CARTHEW MINOR FROM THE NORTH END OF CAMERON LAKE.
THE ROUTE IS APPROXIMATE.
SL=DIRECTION OF SUMMIT LAKE. CM=CARTHEW MINOR.

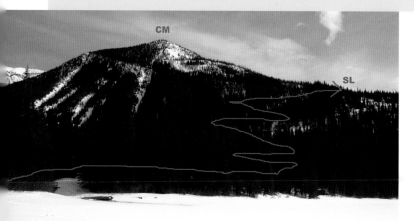

The terrain steepens higher up on the hillside. Here, it will be very difficult to make separate ski and snowshoe trails. Sharing the same trail may be necessary.

The terrain eventually starts to level out. If Summit Lake is your destination, snowshoe southeast over the lightly treed terrain. A minor elevation loss will be required to make it to the shore of the lake (GR175326). The lake grants decent views of Chapman Peak and Mount Custer in Glacier National Park. Return the same way if you are done for the day.

### Onward to Carthew Minor

Carthew Minor lies due north of Summit Lake. From Summit Lake, an additional 400 m of vertical elevation gain is required for this ascent. Although it is not necessary to visit Summit Lake to get to Carthew Minor, the diversion is worthwhile and a minimum of effort is required.

From the lake, snowshoe north to intercept the south ridge of the peak. Trend very slightly to the right as you go. Soon the terrain to your right starts to fall away into the valley below. This is a good indication you are heading in the right direction. Don't lose any elevation; just keep going north and up.

The trees start to thin and a path up the outlier becomes visible. There are some deceptively steep slopes ahead (35°), so be prepared for them with aggressive snowshoe crampons or foot crampons (**avalanche danger**). In the right conditions, step-kicking up these slopes without snowshoes or crampons may also be a possibility. However, the snow was like brick on my February 2010 ascent, and step-kicking was not an option. My MSR Lightning Ascent snowshoes worked like a dream on that day.

Aim for a prominent and distinctive pillar of red rock, visible from low down. On the way up, monitor snow conditions carefully and retreat if there are signs of a potential avalanche. Past the interesting rock pillar, there is one more steep slope to ascend (**avalanche danger**). Again, it doesn't look like much from afar, but when you start up you'll know you are on steep terrain. Beyond the main ascent slope, easier terrain leads quickly to the summit at GR177339.

The best views from the top lie to the south in Glacier National Park. Undoubtedly, the beautiful form of Mount Custer, with statuesque Kintla and Kinnerly to the right, will command most of your attention. Glacier's tallest peak, Mount Cleveland, and several surrounding pinnacle-like peaks are also prominent to the southeast. On our side of the fence, Alderson and Carthew look very pleasant (and tempting!). Farther west, straddling the Alberta–British Columbia boundary, sits Forum Peak, with Akamina Ridge beyond. These peaks will likely be holding far more snow than their counterparts in Alberta.

Return the same way. **Do not** attempt to take a more direct route down, as the lower slopes are considerably steeper. Once back at the switchbacks, point your snowshoes downhill and enjoy a fast and hopefully exhilarating plunge-stepping ride down to the lake. It is not necessary to follow your uptrack down, but of course that is also an option.

AN ETHEREAL VIEW OF MOUNT CUSTER (RIGHT)
FROM THE SUMMIT OF CARTHEW MINOR.

# 4 FORUM RIDGE

(MAP 1, PAGE 312)

| | |
|---|---|
| DIFFICULTY | MODERATE |
| HAZARD | LOW |
| RIDGE HEIGHT | 2230+ M |
| ELEVATION GAIN | 570+ M |
| ROUND-TRIP DISTANCE | 10 KM |
| ROUND-TRIP TIME | 5–6 HOURS |
| MAPS | 82 G/1 SAGE CREEK, GEM TREK WATERTON LAKES NATIONAL PARK |

*For a stellar view of Cameron Lake and the magnificent east face of Mount Custer, Forum Ridge is the ticket! The route to the ridge is fairly straightforward, although very steep in one section. Hardcore mountaineers can continue on to the summit of Forum Peak. Don't try the route too early in the season. If the snow is deep and unconsolidated, ascending "the big hill" may be next to impossible.*

## DIRECTIONS

Follow Cameron Lake Road to the blockade, park, and start snowshoeing or hiking the well-packed road. About 1.5 km along, turn right onto the signed Akamina Pass trail. This trail is well used and will probably also be packed down. Follow the wide trail for 1.5 km to Akamina Pass. Right before the bulletin board, the boundary park cutline heads southeast into the trees. Follow the cutline for a few hundred metres, after which the cutline takes a sharp right, now heading southwest. Stay on the cutline. You'll lose a little elevation before being confronted by "the big hill." It looks steep and it is, approaching 45° for a very short section.

Getting up the hill is the crux of the trip. Either tackle it head-on or make switchbacks across the slope. Some will try to avoid the steepness of the hill by swinging far to the east side of the ridge and looking for less-steep slopes back to the cutline. Choose your poison!

Atop the hill, continue following the cutline, still going southwest. The trees soon thin and the view starts to open up. To experience the view, follow the ridge at least until you are out of the trees. On a clear day, the east face of Mount Custer is absolutely stunning. Shapely Chapman Peak to the left of Custer is nothing to sneeze at either. Cameron Lake below and the daunting north face of Forum Peak also make this viewpoint a very satisfying one.

No need to stop yet. You can safely follow the ridge to within a few hundred metres of Forum's north face. Beyond that, the ridge starts to narrow and becomes a little more exposed. Snowshoe to a point that doesn't compromise your comfort level, and then consider your descent route.

ON FORUM RIDGE, WITH FORUM PEAK TO THE RIGHT, MOUNT CHAPMAN AT THE FAR LEFT AND MOUNT CUSTER TO THE RIGHT OF CHAPMAN.

Returning the way you came is an easy affair. However, an alternative descent down the east side of the ridge to Cameron Lake has great appeal. Return along the ridge to reach treeline. As you traverse the ridge, look for a descent route down the east side of the ridge that you feel comfortable on. It is possible to descend open slopes that are not treed, but this is obvious avalanche terrain (**avalanche danger**). If you and your party are properly equipped and the avalanche hazard is low, go for it! Otherwise, it's much better to play it safe and descend through the trees to Cameron Lake. At the lake, follow Cameron Lakeshore Trail to the north end of Cameron Lake or take a direct route across the lake to the north end (provided, of course, it's frozen). It's about 2.5 km back to your vehicle from the end of the lake.

THE STELLAR VIEW OF MOUNT CUSTER, AS SEEN FROM FORUM RIDGE.

# 5 FORUM PEAK

(MAP 1, PAGE 312)

> DIFFICULTY DIFFICULT, MOUNTAINEERING
> HAZARD HIGH
> MOUNTAIN HEIGHT 2415 M
> ELEVATION GAIN 780 M
> ROUND-TRIP DISTANCE 13–15 KM
> ROUND-TRIP TIME 8–10 HOURS
> MAPS 82 G/1 SAGE CREEK,
> GEM TREK WATERTON LAKES NATIONAL PARK

*This trip just might afford one of the most scenic winter viewpoints in the Canadian Rockies. The views are breathtaking in every direction from the top of Forum Peak, especially to the south. Our March 2010 ascent still stands out in my memory as one of the most rewarding trips we've ever completed. This route is for mountaineers only. An ice axe and crampons are mandatory, and most will feel the need for a climbing rope and a few slings for protection. Avalanche gear is also mandatory. For those who want to make the summit without the difficult mountaineering sections, follow the alternative descent route described below.*

## DIRECTIONS

Follow the directions for Forum Ridge (see page 92). When you reach the section where the ridge starts to narrow, put away your snowshoes and continue on foot or, better yet, with crampons and an axe. Take your snowshoes with you, especially if you plan to take the alternative descent route. Carefully follow the ridge to the rock face, being cognizant of cornices on the left and avalanche concerns on the right (**avalanche danger**). From here, the

scramble route goes around the right side of the rock-band and then ascends a weakness back to the ridge. However, in winter this route is extremely dangerous because of avalanche issues (**severe avalanche danger**). Unless the snow has melted away (unlikely, given the north orientation of the slope), the scramble route should be completely avoided.

Instead, traverse a few metres around the left side of the rock face, looking for a route up. Even the least steep route requires a few low-fifth-class moves. A rope and protection (slings) are strongly recommended here. Gain the nose of the ridge and then traverse around the right side for a few metres and then up to a flatter plateau. Again, expect fifth-class moves and exposure. Once you've started up this rock-band, it will be difficult to back down.

From the plateau, easier terrain leads to a very large summit cairn. On the way up, you may have to traverse out to the right, away from the ridge for some sections. This will put you on avalanche-prone slopes – use discretion.

When you reach the cairn, you'll be glad you made the effort.

ABOVE: THE VIEW SOUTH
INTO GLACIER NATIONAL
PARK FROM THE SUMMIT
OF FORUM PEAK.
RIGHT: THE CRUX
SECTION OF FORUM
PEAK. A=AVALANCHE
SLOPES TO AVOID.

The view is phenomenal, especially the striking forms of Kinnerly and Kintla, in Glacier National Park. Wander over to a couple of other highpoints to the south for even better views.

The fastest descent route is the same way you came. Getting down the rock-band will probably require a rappel (50-m rope).

The alternative descent via the ridge between Wall and Forum lakes is the preferred route. Snowshoe west to the first, rounded highpoint west of Forum Peak. It may be very tempting to continue west along scenic Akamina Ridge. This is definitely a possibility for those who still have the lots of energy and are equipped

ATOP FORUM PEAK: THE MAGNIFICENT VIEW TO
THE WEST AND THE ALTERNATIVE DESCENT ROUTE.
LK=LONG KNIFE PEAK. AR=SUMMIT OF AKAMINA RIDGE.

with avalanche gear. For everyone else, turn north at the high-point and follow the wide ridge down. It soon narrows a little and gets steeper. Other than a few minor detours to the right to get around small rock steps, there are no difficulties toward the low col. However, this terrain is definitely steep enough to avalanche.

Descend the ridge all the way to the col or until it starts veering off to the right (east), down into the basin below (**avalanche danger**). This is terrific glissading terrain. As you descend, note the location of Forum Lake. The lake is a fairly popular destination,

and there may be snowshoe trails to follow down to Akamina Pass Trail. Upon reaching the basin, snowshoe northeast to eventually intercept one of the possible trails mentioned above (it is not necessary to snowshoe to Forum Lake, unless you really want to). If no trail has been broken, snowshoe to the creek emanating from Forum Lake, cross it and then go in a more northerly direction to eventually hit Akamina Pass Trail. Turn right onto the trail and follow it up to Akamina Pass and then easily back to your vehicle.

**Note** The alternative descent route described above can be used in reverse as an ascent route to Forum Peak and/or Akamina Ridge. This route eliminates the difficult mountaineering sections, but it still ascends avalanche slopes. Avalanche gear is mandatory and crampons and an ice axe are useful in steeper sections.

# HIGHWAY 774 (CASTLE CROWN)

*The Castle Crown area, north of Waterton Lakes National Park, is home to the Castle Mountain Ski Resort. Not surprisingly, the area receives a large amount of snow, though often a few weeks later than parts of the Rockies farther north. Like Waterton, snowshoeing opportunities are minimal, though the adventurous snowshoer can find somewhere interesting to explore in almost any area.*

*If you are a fan of rime (interesting snow and ice formations on trees and rock, caused when super-cooled water droplets freeze*

upon striking an object) or hoarfrost, the Castle Crown and Waterton areas are the places to be. High winds can whip the snow and ice into beautiful and striking forms. The price of seeing these phenomena usually involves gaining enough elevation to areas where they are present – a mountaintop or summit ridge.

To this day, Victoria Ridge/Peak and "Middle Kootenay Mountain" remain as two of my favourite trips of all time. As a curious note, my brother, Mark, and I took snowshoes for both of these trips but didn't have to use them.

"MIDDLE KOOTENAY MOUNTAIN."

# 6 "MIDDLE KOOTENAY MOUNTAIN"

(MAP 2, PAGE 313)

| | |
|---|---|
| DIFFICULTY | MODERATE TO FALSE SUMMIT, DIFFICULT TO TRUE SUMMIT |
| HAZARD | MODERATE TO FALSE SUMMIT, HIGH TO TRUE SUMMIT |
| MOUNTAIN HEIGHT | 2512 M |
| ELEVATION GAIN | FIRST SUMMIT 1100 M, TRUE SUMMIT 1200 M |
| ROUND-TRIP DISTANCE | APPROX. 22 KM |
| ROUND-TRIP TIME | 10–12 HOURS |
| ADDITIONAL EQUIPMENT | AVALANCHE GEAR, CRAMPONS, ICE AXE |
| MAPS | 82 G/08 BEAVER MINES |

*A winter ascent of "Middle Kootenay Mountain" is a long affair. The scenery along the route and from the summit is absolutely breathtaking. Do not go near this mountain unless clear skies are a guarantee. Our January 2009 ascent was as unforgettable an experience in the mountains as we've ever had. Get a very early start, bring a headlamp and be prepared to expend a significant amount of energy to make it to the summit. There are several highpoints and a false summit that serve as great consolation prizes if you come up short of the true summit. The 8-km approach to Middle Kootenay Pass is along a popular snowmobile trail. In the right conditions, it is actually possible to bike about 4 km of this approach, even in the cold winter months. Also, bring a Crazy Carpet to make to descent a little more exhilarating.*

## Directions

Drive toward Castle Mountain Ski Resort but stay left instead of turning right into the parking lot. In a few hundred metres the road turns left to a small bridge. At this point, depending on the time of year, you may be able to drive the next few kilometres, or a snow barricade may be blocking further access. Driving is possible in November and maybe early December. However, as soon as sufficient snow has fallen, this trail becomes a snowmobile route. Do not drive the 2.6-km approach if the trail is already obviously in use as a snowmobile route. Instead, park at the barricade and proceed on foot or even bike. Bikes are only recommended when the trail has been well packed down and also in colder temperatures, when daytime warming will not soften the snow.

Regardless of your method of conveyance, bike or hike (snowshoes should not be necessary until you leave the trail) 2.6 km to a major fork in the road (GR890638). Take the right fork, crossing a bridge in short order and another quickly after that. If you are cycling the approach, it is best to leave your bike when the trail turns sharply to the right and starts to gain elevation. However, if you are confident about riding down snow-packed trails and the snow is supportive, consider riding or pushing it farther up the trail.

Follow the wide trail/road for several kilometres until you arrive at a sign warning of avalanche danger for snowmobilers. Throughout the approach be aware that this route is very popular with snowmobilers. Listen for them and remember to always move completely off the trail to allow them to pass. Moving only to the side of the trail is not enough.

You will come to a noticeable sign on a tree that details the route. If the avalanche danger is high, follow the lower trail to the left. If not, go right, heading up steeper terrain. Leave the

snowshoes on your pack for faster travel if the snow is supportive. You'll eventually go through an open gate or have to walk
around it if it's locked. As the scenery begins to open up, note
the first section of your objective, which first appears directly
ahead of you and then to the right. The long ridge to the left is
part of Rainy Ridge.

Although it is not necessary to continue all the way to Middle
Kootenay Pass, the route from the pass is the least steep option
and therefore less prone to avalanches, if the slopes are snow-
covered. The pass sits about 200 m from the point where the trail
descends a small slope. From the pass, leave the trail and head
to your right (northwest), up open slopes. These slopes are fairly
steep at the bottom and crampons and an ice axe (or good crampons on your snowshoes) may be necessary if the snow is hard.
Use discretion if avalanches are a possibility (**avalanche danger**).

The southwest slopes are subject to strong winds and may be the most snow-free option. After gaining some elevation, the grade becomes more manageable, but it's still a fair distance up the foreshortened slope to the first summit.

Most of the remainder of the trip can be seen from summit one. Take note of your ascent time to this point, as well as your energy level. Call it a day if the first is in abundance, the second not so much. To continue, simply follow the ridge heading west, over another highpoint and then on to the main section of the mountain. A couple of minor rock-bands high on the mountain are easily scrambled up and over. The false summit, at GR863600, sports a terrific view and again may be enough for many.

THE EASY AND HIGHLY ENJOYABLE RIDGE, AS SEEN FROM THE FIRST SUMMIT. FS=FALSE SUMMIT. TSS=TRUE SUMMIT — SOUTH PEAK.

The true summit lies about 500 m to the west and is approximately 20 vertical m higher. The view includes a good look at Tombstone Mountain and is definitely worthwhile if you have the time and inclination. This is the most dangerous part of the trip, though, and those who continue down to the col between the false and true summits should be confident about assessing avalanche conditions and descending steep, snowy terrain.

Follow the ridge down a short distance to a drop-off. Go left and find a weakness down through this rock-band. Repeat this procedure several times in order to get down to the col between the false and true summits. This loss may be tricky if the terrain is snow-covered, requiring crampons and an ice axe. If the area is snow-covered, staying close to the ridge is the safest option but is also more difficult and exposed. Beware of the cornice to your right. Trending left onto snow-covered slopes is not recommended if there is any risk of an avalanche (**severe avalanche danger**).

From the col follow the ridge easily to the summit. You will encounter a rock-band just before the top, but it is easily scrambled up, around the left side. The first summit is only a couple of minutes from the rock-band. Take in an excellent view and then traverse about 200 m south to the other summit (only about 5 minutes away). These two summits are of comparable height and both warrant a visit.

Return the same way. Back at the col below the true summit, side-sloping on the south side of the mountain to avoid regaining all the highpoints again can save a fair amount of time and energy, but only do this if the slopes are safe to traverse. When you are just below Middle Kootenay Pass, take out the Crazy Carpet and enjoy a good ride down. The flat final 4 km will probably be very tiring.

SNOW-ENCASED TREES IN JANUARY,
NEAR THE SUMMIT, ON A PERFECT DAY.

# 7 "LITTLE MIDDLE KOOTENAY PEAK"

(MAP 2, PAGE 313)

| | |
|---|---|
| DIFFICULTY | EASY BUT LONG |
| HAZARD | MODERATE |
| MOUNTAIN HEIGHT | 2280 M |
| ELEVATION GAIN | 850 M |
| ROUND-TRIP DISTANCE | 16 KM |
| ROUND-TRIP TIME | 5–8 HOURS |
| ADDITIONAL EQUIPMENT | AVALANCHE GEAR |
| MAP | 82 G/8 BEAVER MINES |

*This unofficially named peak, east of unofficially named Middle Kootenay Mountain, boasts a terrific view of the southeast side of Mount Haig, as well as other peaks in the area. It is a shorter and easier alternative to Middle Kootenay Mountain, but the approach is still long. Thankfully, for most of the trip, a snowmobile-packed trail helps to make travel less strenuous.*

## DIRECTIONS

Most of the approach is the same as "Middle Kootenay Mountain" (see page 102). Drive toward Castle Mountain Ski Resort, but stay left instead of turning right into the parking lot. In a few hundred metres the road turns left to a small bridge. At this point, depending on the time of year, you may be able to drive the next few kilometres, or a snow barricade may be blocking further access. Driving is possible in November and maybe early December. However, as soon as sufficient snow has fallen, this trail becomes a snowmobile route. Do not drive the 2.6-km approach if the trail is already obviously in use as a snowmobile route. Instead, park at the barricade and proceed on foot or even bike. Bikes are only recommended when the trail has been well packed down and also in colder temperatures when daytime warming will not soften the snow.

Regardless of your method of travel, hike (snowshoes should not be necessary until you leave the trail) 2.6 km to a major fork in the road (GR890638). Take the right fork, crossing a bridge in short order and another quickly after that. Follow the wide trail/road for several kilometres until you arrive at a sign warning of avalanche danger for snowmobilers. Throughout the approach be aware that this route is very popular with snowmobilers. Listen for them and remember to always move completely off the trail to allow them to pass. Moving only to the side of the trail is not enough.

You will come to a noticeable sign on a tree that details the route. If the avalanche danger is high, follow the lower trail to the left, as suggested. If not, go right, heading up steeper terrain. If the snow is supportive, leave your snowshoes on your pack so you can travel faster. The lower slopes of Little Middle are now on your right. Do not be tempted to ascend these slopes too early, however, as they are steep and avalanche-prone. Instead, continue following the trail toward Middle Kootenay Pass. At about GR888608, 1730 m, 20–30 minutes after passing the sign, look for relatively open and gently graded slopes to your right. Put on your snowshoes and leave the trail here, heading upslope in a WNW direction.

After gaining some elevation, most of the remaining route should become visible (see photo A on next page). Make your way up to the ridge. Once there, unless you want to experience terminal velocity first-hand, don't stray too far onto the cornice overhanging the north face. Follow the ridge west to the summit at GR872611, 2280 m. The summit is treed, but the trees do not impair the terrific view. Of note in the summit panorama are the southeast side of Mount Haig, the false summit of Middle Kootenay Mountain to the southwest, and Barnaby Ridge stretched out to the east. Return the same way. With good snow conditions, the downhill sections of the descent are fast and easy. Once back on the trail, a Crazy Carpet is useful for the steep sections.

[A] THE EASY EAST RIDGE OF LITTLE MIDDLE KOOTENAY PEAK.

# 8 VICTORIA RIDGE

(MAP 3, PAGE 314)

| | |
|---|---|
| DIFFICULTY MODERATE | |
| HAZARD MODERATE | |
| MOUNTAIN HEIGHT 2512 M | |
| ELEVATION GAIN 1000 M | |
| ROUND-TRIP DISTANCE 26 KM | |
| ROUND-TRIP TIME 8–12 HOURS | |
| ADDITIONAL EQUIPMENT AVALANCHE GEAR, CRAMPONS AND ICE AXE IF SNOWY CONDITIONS | |
| MAPS 82 G/08 BEAVER MINES | |

*Victoria Ridge really doesn't qualify as a snowshoe trip, but it is my favourite ridgewalk and worth a visit at any time of the year. The trip's significant distance (both horizontal and vertical) is more conducive to a summer or fall ascent, but early spring is also an option, subject to snow conditions. The colours of rock are amazing throughout, so the best time to do the ascent is when enough snow has melted to reveal those colours but some still remains to enhance the surrounding scenery. Bikes are great for the first 4 km, and hopefully snowshoes will only be needed in the valley, if at all. April can be a good month to get the right conditions. If the snow is deep and unsupportive throughout, making the summit will not be possible. If that's the case, pick a more feasible objective.*

## DIRECTIONS

This trip is accessed from Highway 6, south of Pincher Creek, not Highway 774 as the title of this section of trips suggests. From Pincher Creek, head south toward Waterton. About 20.5 km south of the south end of Pincher Creek, take Highway 505 west

*ABOVE: VIBRANT COLOURS OF A LATE-SPRING ASCENT.
VICTORIA PEAK AT THE FAR RIGHT.
RIGHT: [A] THE DISTANT GR ON VICTORIA RIDGE, AS SEEN FROM
THE APPROACH ROAD. NOTE THE AMOUNT OF SNOW ON THE TRAVERSE
SLOPES. VP=VICTORIA PEAK. GR=DISTANT GR. TS=TRAVERSE SLOPES.*

(the east turnoff comes up first – don't take it!). Follow the 505 for 9.2 km and turn left at the "Forest Reserve" sign, onto TWP RD 4-3. Drive 5.5 km to the Victoria Ridge trailhead. You may have to park outside the gates, about 50 m before the locked gate.

Hike or bike the gravel road for 4 km until it stops and becomes a trail. En route take note of the distant GR to the left of Victoria Peak (see photo A). The route traverses the lower slopes of this GR, and if it is plastered in snow, travel may be very dangerous due

[B] *The distinctive GR on Victoria Ridge.*

to the steep grade and potential avalanches. Leave your bike at the end of the trail and hike or snowshoe along the pleasant trail through the valley, going southwest. Pincher Creek lies to the left. The aforementioned, distinctive GR in front of you can be used as a reference for navigation if the trail is difficult to follow.

In short, the route ascends treed terrain to a point northeast of the GR and then turns south, traversing the lower east face of the GR. Keep this in mind as you continue up the valley.

When the creek turns to the south, the trail curves right, heading uphill through the trees (approximately GR080622). Higher up, the trail goes left under the impressive walls of one of the aforementioned GR (see photo B) and then goes south a short distance below the ridge and parallel to it. These slopes can be steep to traverse. If the snow is hard, an ice axe will be the minimum requirement and crampons a good idea.

When you are a fair distance past the summit of the GR, it is best to turn right and ascend easy slopes to the ridge. Again, an ice axe will be very useful here. It is more scenic on this route than it would be if you had remained on the trail below the ridge, but it requires additional elevation losses and gains. Once on the ridge, turn left and head south toward the highpoint of the ridge some distance away (see photo C). You will have to drop to a low col below before making the final push to the summit of Victoria Ridge. Be sure to stop occasionally and enjoy the colourful views of Pincher Ridge. Return the same way, but follow the directions below to get the most out of the trip by traversing a portion of the ridge toward Victoria Peak.

### North route on the ridgetop

If you don't feel like completing the long ridgewalk all the way to the summit of Victoria Ridge, gain the ridge as discussed above and then turn north instead of south. The first, cairned highpoint is easily gained. Continue north along the jagged ridge,

[C] LINDA BRETON ON THE RIDGE CONNECTING VICTORIA PEAK TO THE SUMMIT OF VICTORIA RIDGE. VR=SUMMIT OF VICTORIA RIDGE.

which now has a precipitous drop on the right. You can easily circumnavigate a few small drop-offs by dropping down to the left a short distance. Upon reaching the next and most prominent highpoint, the ridge descends to a low col that separates Victoria Ridge from Victoria Peak. If you have the energy, it's a straightforward scree/rubble ascent to the summit of Victoria Peak from here. If not, pick one of several descent routes back to the trail (see photo D). Avalanches are a concern for these descent routes, but by mid-April they may be snow-free.

[D] THERE ARE MANY CHOICES FOR DESCENT. C=LOW COL. VP=SUMMIT OF VICTORIA PEAK. V=VALLEY. H=THE HIGH-DESCENT ROUTE.

# HIGHWAY 541

Highway 541 is the south section of Highway 40. It starts at Longview and then runs west for about 45 km to a closed gate just beyond the Highway 940 turnoff. Because this is a Front Range area, peaks and routes can be snow-free during any month of the year, or they can be absolutely plastered in snow. Snowshoes may or may not be necessary for the three trips that follow. It's always a good idea to take them anyway.

This area may also be subject to clearer skies when cloudy conditions persist to the west. There is a great deal of potential for more snowshoeing routes around Highway 541 and south down Highway 940.

WIND-RAVAGED TREES DOMINATE THE SCENERY ON BULL CREEK HILLS.

# 9 BULL CREEK HILLS

(MAP 4, PAGE 315)

DIFFICULTY MODERATE

HAZARD MODERATE FOR THE LOOP ROUTE

MOUNTAIN HEIGHT 2179 M

ELEVATION GAIN 750 M

ROUND-TRIP DISTANCE 8–12 KM

ROUND-TRIP TIME 6–9 HOURS

ADDITIONAL EQUIPMENT AVALANCHE GEAR FOR THE DESCENT VIA FIR CREEK, AS A PRECAUTION

MAPS 82 J/7 MOUNT HEAD, GEM TREK HIGHWOOD AND CATARACT CREEK

*These hills make for a great day out at any time of the year. The area is subject to very high winds, so watch for wind-loaded slopes and retreat if the winds are too strong. Violent gusts have been known to knock people off their feet. There are many routes to the summit, including ones via Grass Pass, Fir Creek and slopes near Marston Creek. Described below is the ascent near Marston Creek and a descent via Fir Creek.*

## DIRECTIONS

From Longview, drive about 35 km west on Highway 541 and park just off the road at the Highwood River Recreation parking lot. Cross the road and start heading north. There is a trail, but snow cover may make it difficult to locate. There is a small outlier to the right, and you'll want to be west of it. Ascend gentle terrain past this outlier. A barbed-wire fence will let you know if you stray too far east. Eventually, the first major highpoint becomes visible, with the summit in the background to the left of the highpoint. Make your way across open meadows toward the highpoint, quickly arriving at a stand of trees. At this point the trail swings sharply to the right and down before resuming its northward direction. Cross Marston Creek and emerge from the trees, again heading north. Ascend another hill, at which point the main ascent slope will become visible.

Once on the correct ascent slope, directions are unnecessary. Simply follow the terrain up to the first highpoint. From there the wide ridge descends a little, curving around to the west. Follow the ridge to the highest point of Bull Creek Hills, at 2179 m.

To descend, either return the same way or complete a loop route via Fir Creek or Grass Pass. For the two latter routes, continue west, from the summit down to the next highpoint, about 500 m away. The highpoint farther west of this one is also easily reached. The Fir Creek valley should now be visible to the southwest.

### Fir Creek descent
Continue following the ridge or line of least resistance to get to

THE WINDBLASTED SLOPES OF BULL CREEK HILLS, AS SEEN FROM NEAR THE BEGINNING OF THE TRIP. FH=FIRST HIGHPOINT. S=SUMMIT.

a point directly north of the Fir Creek valley. Descend south into the valley. Some of the slopes are steep enough to avalanche under the right conditions (**avalanche danger**). Use discretion. Once in the valley, follow open meadows alongside Fir Creek, mostly on the east side. Farther down the valley, stay on the east side as you approach the trees. There is a narrow trail that winds through the trees, and you should do your best to find it. Look for occasional flagging. This trail stays fairly high above the creek and leads easily back to the road. Finish the loop with a 2-km hike along the road back to your vehicle.

### Grass Pass descent

This route makes for a fairly long day and adds about 4 km to the shorter Fir Creek Descent. Follow the Fir Creek Descent route but don't descend into Fir Creek valley. Instead, continue SSW along the ridge. It soon turns west and drops down to Grass Pass at GR714875. A good trail, 3.2 km in length, goes south to the highway. It's another 3 km back to your vehicle from the Grass Pass trailhead.

*A VERY WINDY AUTUMN DAY ON BULL CREEK HILLS.*

# 10 COYOTE HILL

(MAP 4, PAGE 315)

DIFFICULTY MODERATE

HAZARD LOW IF THE SAFEST ROUTE IS TAKEN,
OTHERWISE MODERATE

MOUNTAIN HEIGHT 2140 M

ELEVATION GAIN 540 M

ROUND-TRIP DISTANCE 8.5–10 KM

ROUND-TRIP TIME 4–6 HOURS

MAPS 82 J/7 MOUNT HEAD,
GEM TREK HIGHWOOD AND CATARACT CREEK

*This minor summit at GR652812 (2140 m) is the highest point of the Coyote Hills, east of Mount Armstrong. The top grants a very respectable view of peaks on the Continental Divide, as well as the Highwood Range to the north. It is a good alternative for those who have ascended nearby and slightly higher Junction Hill. There are two routes to the summit. The snow conditions will largely determine which route you should take. If the snow is deep and unconsolidated, Baril Creek Trail may be packed down and easier to travel on. However, a more direct route to the summit is preferable if conditions warrant it. Both routes start from the same parking area.*

## DIRECTIONS

From Longview, drive 45 km west on Highway 541 and turn left onto Highway 940. Drive 3.3 km south on Highway 940 and park on the west (right) side of the road in a small clearing. An unsigned unofficial trail goes up and over the small hill at the northwest end of the parking area, through a short stint of trees, and then intersects the main Baril Creek trail. Simply follow the blue paint markers on the trees from the parking area to Baril Creek Trail.

## DIRECT ROUTE VIA SOUTHEAST SLOPES (RECOMMENDED)

*This route gains elevation sooner than the Baril Creek Trail route and is slightly more scenic. Though the initial views aren't what you would characterize as "spectacular," they should be enough to divert your attention through a few sections of tedious plodding. Before ascending the main peak, this route visits a small outlier east of the summit, necessitating a 60-m elevation loss and regain.*

### DIRECTIONS

Upon reaching the official Baril Creek Trail (frequented by snowmobilers later in the season), hike or snowshoe the trail west for about 10 minutes. In this time the route will descend toward Baril Creek. When the trail reaches its low point at GR678807 (after which it ascends to the left), leave the trail and turn right (north) toward Baril Creek. Descend a steep but short slope to the creek and cross it, taking care to first test the strength of the ice.

Gain the north bank of Baril Creek and continue heading west for another 10 minutes, paralleling the creek. You are now southeast of the objective. Look for a decent place to start up the main section of the peak. Again, turn right (NNW) and ascend the easy and sparsely treed slopes up to the first highpoint of the day at GR670809, 1752 m.

From this highpoint, two outliers of Coyote Hill are visible. If your motivation is waning, the rocky outlier to the north makes a decent consolation prize (see photo A). Simply follow the ridge north to the summit. Views of Holy Cross Mountain and Mount

Head are good, but the summit panorama pales in comparison to that of Coyote Hill. Return the same way.

The second outlier, due west, provides the gateway to Coyote Hill. Hike west up more treed slopes to that highpoint at GR664809, 1886 m. The remainder of the route now becomes clear. The goal is to intercept the south ridge of Coyote Hill and then go north to the summit (see photo B). Lose 60 m of elevation to the col and then slog your way up to the ridge. This is the most strenuous and tedious part of the route. Avalanches, in general, are not a concern until you near the ridge. If snow conditions are stable, pick open areas to ascend. Close to the ridge the terrain does get a little steeper and could slide (**avalanche danger**). As well, later in the season, large cornices may have developed over the ridge and should be steered clear of. If snow conditions are questionable, stay in the trees to the right.

While views of Holy Cross Mountain and Mount Head, to the northeast, have probably been good throughout the trip, the real view is experienced upon reaching the south ridge. The

[A] THE NORTHERN OUTLIER, AS SEEN FROM GR760809.

[B] *THE MAIN ASCENT SLOPES, AS SEEN FROM GR664809. S=SUMMIT.*

"in-your-face" look at Mount Armstrong is particularly impressive. Pyramidal Mount McPhail farther north, along with Strachan and Muir, should look great, plastered in snow.

The summit is about 300–400 m north and the ridgewalk there shouldn't present any challenges. From the top, take in a fine view and then pick one of two descent routes:

Return the same way you came in (recommended). The primary advantage of this option is that you get to follow your own tracks out. The 60 m of elevation regain back to the outlier is a small price to pay for ease of descent.

Alternatively, return via the south ridge. This route is steeper than the southeast slopes and does require stable snow conditions. Other than for variety's sake, and to increase exposure to the view to the west, this route probably won't appeal to those who have ascended via the southeast slopes. Simply follow the ridge south. Carefully assess snow conditions along the way. At the bottom, cross Baril Creek and then slog your way back up to Baril Creek Trail. A somewhat boring 3.5-km hike/snowshoe leads back to the parking area.

## BARIL CREEK TRAIL VIA SOUTH RIDGE ROUTE

*This route is not completely without merit. It does grant fantastic views to the west as soon as some elevation is gained. The other benefit of this route is that much of the horizontal distance is completed along Baril Creek Trail. More than likely the trail will be well packed down and easy to follow. A good compromise is to use the south ridge for ascent and then the southeast slopes for descent.*

*While the slopes of the south ridge are never too steep, they are steep enough to avalanche when the hazard is considerable or higher. Use discretion if choosing this route.*

### DIRECTIONS

Find Baril Creek Trail as described above. Hike or snowshoe approximately 3.5 km along the trail to a point directly south of the south ridge, around GR660793, plus or minus a couple of hundred metres. Look for the line of least resistance to descend to the creek, cross it and then gain the south ridge. This may require some routefinding and/or bushwhacking. Upon reaching the south ridge, follow it north to the summit. Assess snow conditions continually as you ascend. The 500 vertical m of ascent will not be a pushover, but views to the west will give you a good excuse to stop and take a breather. The grade eventually decreases and the final 800 horizontal m to the summit are much easier.

If ascending the south ridge was easy, then returning the same way is definitely a good and probably expedient option. Equally enjoyable is to descend the gentler southeast slopes as follows. Go back along the ridge for about 350 m to a point where you can see directly down open slopes on the east side of the mountain. These slopes are a little steeper near the top, but they are much easier once some elevation is lost. With good snow conditions, plunge-stepping with snowshoes down these slopes is fast and fun. Note the treeless outlier directly east – that's what you are aiming for.

Descend to the col between the main body of Coyote Hill and the outlier and then gain 60 vertical m to the top of the outlier. Another hill appears to the east of the outlier. Descend treed slopes to that hill and then make your way southeast, down to Baril Creek. Cross the creek and find Baril Creek Trail for an easy finish.

# 11 JUNCTION HILL

(MAP 4, PAGE 315)

| | |
|---|---|
| DIFFICULTY MODERATE | |
| HAZARD MODERATE | |
| MOUNTAIN HEIGHT 2236 M | |
| ELEVATION GAIN 720 M | |
| ROUND-TRIP DISTANCE 9 KM | |
| ROUND-TRIP TIME 5–7 HOURS | |
| ADDITIONAL EQUIPMENT AVALANCHE GEAR, AS A PRECAUTION | |
| MAPS 82 J/7 MOUNT HEAD, GEM TREK HIGHWOOD AND CATARACT CREEK | |

*Junction Hill is subject to strong chinook winds and huge doses of sun. Therefore it can be snow-free in any month of the year. Snowshoes may or may not be necessary, but take them just in case. The southeast ridge may be the best route to the summit, but it is not conducive to a snowshoe ascent. The recommended route goes up open slopes on the east side of the southwest ridge and then up treed slopes to the summit. The summit view is very pleasant and quite similar to that of Coyote Hill to the south.*

## DIRECTIONS

From Longview, drive 45 km on Highway 541 to the closed gate (the gate is closed from December 1–June 15). Don't park in front of the gate. Snowshoe or hike on the road for about 600 m past the gate to the green sign that indicates Kananaskis Village is 78 km away. Turn right (north) and start up open slopes, picking the easiest or most interesting line (see photo next page). The exposed rock outcrops to the left are a little out of the way but they provide some interesting scenery and colours.

Make your way up to the first highpoint (approximately GR658853). Sections of terrain here are steep enough to slide, but, as mentioned above, the slopes do not hold snow for long periods of time, reducing the possibility that avalanche-prone slabs will develop. Nevertheless, the possibility does exist (**avalanche danger**). Use all necessary precautions.

The summit is just visible to the north from the first high-point. Take in good views of peaks in the direction of the Continental Divide before continuing. Mounts Armstrong, Strachan and Muir are quite prominent, but the pyramidal form of Mount McPhail is particularly striking. Much of the remainder of the ascent is up forested terrain and lacking in decent views.

A TYPICAL WINTER VIEW OF THE EAST SIDE
OF JUNCTION HILL'S SOUTHWEST SLOPES.
IR=INTERESTING ROCK OUTCROPS. HP=FIRST HIGHPOINT.

Routefinding your way to the summit is straightforward. Follow the ridge north up to the next treed highpoint. A minor elevation loss follows and then it's up again to the next treed highpoint. A second elevation loss after this highpoint may at first feel discouraging, but it too is minor. This terrain does not bear the brunt of the warm winds. The snow could be deep here, in which case your snowshoes will come in handy.

After the second elevation loss, continue north toward the summit. Expect a long stint through the trees, with limited views. The summit, however, offers a front-row view of the west faces of Mount Head and Holy Cross Mountain as well as excellent views of Baril, Armstrong, Strachan, Muir and McPhail.

If the southeast ridge is generally snow-free, it makes an interesting descent route. There's only one way to go – southeast. Go all the way to the end of the ridge and then take a sharp right (west) and routefind your way down to the road. These slopes are quite steep. If covered in hard snow, crampons may be necessary.

Of course, returning the way you came in is also an option.

# HIGHWAY 40 (940) SOUTH

*Highway 40 south does not boast the sheer number of snow-shoe routes that its counterpart to the west does – Highway 742 (Smith-Dorrien) (see page 142). Nevertheless, there are several worthwhile trips in the area and, like Highway 541 (see page 117), the easterly location of this road makes it a good place to find good weather. This is especially true of the north section of the road, which may be basking in sunlight while clouds consume peaks to the west. The north section is also subject to snow-eating blasts from chinook winds. You may*

end up carrying your snowshoes as much as you wear them.

Unfortunately, the best area for snowshoeing along Highway 40 south – the Highwood area – is inaccessible for the majority of the season. Nevertheless, the snow comes early here, and getting in a trip or two before the access road is barricaded on December 1 is often feasible.

On cloudy days, or high avalanche-risk days, you might want to get some exercise by snowshoeing up one of three creeks in the area: Wasootch, Porcupine or King (see the Creeks section of Appendix B, at page 329).

THE SUMMIT VIEW FROM MOUNT KIDD FIRE LOOKOUT.

# 12 MOUNT KIDD LOOKOUT

(MAP 6, PAGE 316)

| | |
|---|---|
| DIFFICULTY | MODERATE |
| HAZARD | LOW–HIGH, DEPENDING ON ROUTE |
| MOUNTAIN HEIGHT | 2128 M |
| ELEVATION GAIN | 600 M |
| ROUND-TRIP DISTANCE | 5.5 KM |
| ROUND-TRIP TIME | 3.5–5 HOURS |
| ADDITIONAL EQUIPMENT | AVALANCHE GEAR, ICE AXE, CRAMPONS (IF NOT ASCENDING THROUGH THE TREES) |
| MAPS | 82 J/14 SPRAY LAKES RESERVOIR, GEM TREK CANMORE |

*The view from this former fire lookout site is somewhat limited, the highpoint being surrounded by much larger peaks. However, even the limited view is spectacular on a clear day. Avoiding avalanche danger involves a strenuous uphill fight through the thick brush. An easier, but potentially more dangerous, option is to ascend slopes adjacent to the avalanche slopes.*

## DIRECTIONS

Driving south on Highway 40, turn right at the Nakiska turnoff. Shortly after, turn left toward Kananaskis Village. Just before the village, turn right at the sign for Mount Kidd Manor and follow the road to the public parking lot. From the lot you'll be able to take in a full view of the ascent slope. It's a good idea to check out the route before you head up (see photo A).

Find the trailhead map at the west end of the parking lot. Two official snowshoe loops are marked on the map. The north loop leads to a three-way intersection with the Aspen and Kovach cross-country ski trails. Follow the loop in either direction toward that signed intersection.

From the intersection, leave the trail and start snowshoeing in a westerly direction. At first, the terrain is easy to negotiate, though you may have to dodge some thicker sections of trees. Within a few hundred metres the slope starts to rise. Work your way up, taking the easiest line. More open terrain lies slightly to the south, but that area will expose you to avalanche slopes. If the avalanche risk is low, ascending slopes to the north of the avalanche slopes is the easiest route to take. This gives you the option to traverse north into the trees and gain gentler slopes, should avalanches become a concern.

Eventually, the trees should thin, and this is where you should make a specific route decision. (If this open terrain doesn't appear, traverse to the left, south, to get to it.) If you are travelling

[A] THE ASCENT ROUTE AS SEEN FROM THE PARKING LOT.
AV=AVALANCHE SLOPES. DR=DIRECT ROUTE. LR=LONG ROUTE.

late in the season, much of the snow may have disappeared from the slopes. In this case you may prefer to pack up your snowshoes and proceed on foot. Pick an ascent line and up you go. Staying near to or in the trees is strongly recommended.

Depending on your ascent line, you may top out right at the former lookout site or just north of it. Traverse south if necessary. The view to the west is very good but not as impressive as the sight of the daunting northeast buttress of Mount Kidd rising sharply to the south. A 5.7 rock route goes right up the centre of this buttress and is described well in Sean Dougherty's *Selected Alpine Climbs*. To get a better view of the climb, follow the ridge south for a few hundred metres to the next highpoint.

To descend, either return the same way if you came through the trees, or take a more direct line (when the avalanche hazard is low) by descending northeast directly from the lookout. Keep heading northeast as you descend and avoid going directly into the avalanche gully unless conditions are really, really safe! Then turn east, going straight down the slopes. With an ice axe, you can glissade these open slopes. The direct route will have you back at your vehicle in about an hour.

RIGHT: *Don't forget to check out the small stuff along the way.*
BELOW: *The north ridge of Mount Kidd.*

# 13 "PACKENHAM JUNIOR"

(MAP 7, PAGE 317)

| | |
|---|---|
| **DIFFICULTY** DIFFICULT | |
| **HAZARD** HIGH | |
| **MOUNTAIN HEIGHT** 2295 M | |
| **ELEVATION GAIN** 600 M | |
| **ROUND-TRIP DISTANCE** 3 KM | |
| **ROUND-TRIP TIME** 3–4 HOURS | |
| **ADDITIONAL EQUIPMENT** AVALANCHE GEAR, CRAMPONS, ICE AXE | |
| **MAPS** 82 J/14 SPRAY LAKES RESERVOIR, 82 J/11 KANANASKIS LAKES, GEM TREK KANANASKIS LAKES | |

*"Packenham Junior," as named by Calvin Damen, is a lowly outlier, lying west of Mount Packenham. However, the views of the Opal Range from this diminutive peak are magnificent on a clear day. While the lower slopes are reasonably gentle in grade, the upper ones are steeper, requiring step-kicking or crampons and an ice axe, not to mention stable snow conditions.*

## DIRECTIONS

Park on the side of the road at the bridge that crosses Hood Creek, about 3 km north of the Kananaskis Lakes turnoff. Be sure your vehicle is well off the road and not blocking traffic. If the snow has not been cleared off the shoulder enough to allow you to park safely, park somewhere else or find another objective.

You could park at the King Creek or Grizzly Creek recreation area, but if you do you will have to walk a fair distance (approximately 3 km from each parking lot) to get to Hood Creek.

From the Hood Creek bridge, much of the route, including the upper slope, is visible (see photo A). Routefinding is as easy as it looks. Basically, follow the southwest edge of the peak to the summit. The summit can be reached from anywhere on the west side, but staying to the south affords good views of mounts Packenham, Hood and Brock, even from low on the slopes. Of course, don't go too far over to the south. The steep slopes falling into Hood Creek could slide (**avalanche danger**), taking you with them .

Continue following the southwest side up, alternating open areas with treed areas. Upon reaching treeline, take your snowshoes off and proceed on foot or with crampons, depending on the snow conditions. The steepest part of the ascent occurs at

[A] THE ASCENT ROUTE UP PACKENHAM JUNIOR, AS SEEN FROM HIGHWAY 40. MOUNT PACKENHAM TO THE RIGHT OF JUNIOR.

the first rock-band, a short distance above treeline – be cautious (**avalanche danger**). Above this section, the grade eases a little but still has slide potential, though minimal. Near the summit, you'll probably intercept the south ridge. A short walk north finishes the ascent.

Take some time to absorb the terrific view of the Opal Range and then return the same way. Other routes down are possible but, because of safety concerns, are not recommended.

MOUNT HOOD, AS SEEN FROM THE ASCENT
SLOPES OF PACKENHAM JUNIOR.

# 14 POCATERRA RIDGE

(MAP 5, PAGE 315)

DIFFICULTY MODERATE

HAZARD MODERATE

MOUNTAIN HEIGHT 2670 M

ELEVATION GAIN 470 M

ROUND-TRIP DISTANCE APPROX. 8 KM

ROUND-TRIP TIME 4–6 HOURS

ADDITIONAL EQUIPMENT AVALANCHE GEAR

MAPS 82 J/14 SPRAY LAKE RESERVOIR,
82 J/11 KANANASKIS LAKES,
GEM TREK KANANASKIS LAKES

*Access to the beautiful Highwood area is limited to June 15–December 1. However, if the snow comes early, there are a number of good trips that can be completed before the gate closes on December 1. At an elevation of 2206 m, Highwood Pass is one of the first areas in the eastern Rockies to receive and retain snow. The odd year will see snow depths reach from 50 cm to a full metre in November.*

*Pocaterra Ridge (not to be confused with nearby Mount Pocaterra) is a popular summer outing and deservedly so. The scenery is excellent and summit views are beautiful. Even if you don't make the summit, the Pocaterra Cirque southeast of the peak is a more than worthy destination.*

## DIRECTIONS

Park at the Highwood Meadows–Ptarmigan Cirque parking lot, just south of Highwood Pass. The majority of this trip travels through open areas, where there is more than enough room for a ski track and a separate snowshoe trail. As always, if a ski track is present, stay off it.

Snowshoe northwest across a small bridge and then out into the open. Continue northwest, paralleling the slopes of Highwood Ridge on the left. Soon the pathway starts to narrow. About 500 m from the parking lot, a large rock (probably snow-covered) sits at the right side of the trail. At this point veer left into the trees. This is the summer trail and hopefully will be obvious. For the next 20–30 minutes this trail heads gently up and through the treed slopes of Highwood Ridge's north end, curving around to the west. There are several narrow sections where it will be necessary to share the ski trail, but only for short distances at a time. The trail ascends for the first half and then gently descends, heading southwest and then west into the open area southeast of Pocaterra Ridge.

Once you are out of the trees, most of the rest of the route is visible (see photo opposite). Continue traversing around the slopes of Highwood Ridge and then northwest to the slopes of the southeast side of Pocaterra Ridge. The objective at this point is to gain the south ridge via whichever route is the safest and/or most feasible. While traversing the lower slopes, going west to intercept the south ridge at a relatively low point is the safest route. More direct routes are possible, depending on the amount and stability of the snow. Once you are on the south ridge, follow it north toward the summit. The grade does steepen for a little while, but it's nothing too alarming. First, you reach a false summit. The true summit is only about 100 m farther, but it may be a dicey proposition in certain snow conditions. Go slowly if snow is piled high on the ridge, and be prepared to forgo the true summit if the traverse is too dangerous.

After enjoying the excellent summit view, return the same way. Continuing north along the ridge is a possibility, if conditions warrant. However, this long traverse is best saved for a summer day and not recommended in the fall, especially if there is a large amount of snow on the ridge. A second car is also required for the traverse – that or a 10-km uphill hike along the road, back to the Highwood Pass.

*THE POPULAR CIRQUE AND SOUTH RIDGE. S=SUMMIT.*

# HIGHWAY 742 (SMITH-DORRIEN)

This stretch of highway from Canmore to the Kananaskis Lakes Trail turnoff is probably the best location in the Canadian Rockies for snowshoeing, especially in the south end. You can park your vehicle almost anywhere along this road and find an interesting route or area to snowshoe in; just don't park in any of the "no stopping" zones, because they are avalanche areas. Returning to find your vehicle buried in several metres of avalanche debris may put a real damper on the day!

The snow here comes early and is often very deep.

MOUNT BIRDWOOD DOMINATES THE VIEW ON AN ASCENT OF SMUTWOOD PEAK.

# 15 "LITTLE LOUGHEED"

(MAP 6, PAGE 316)

| | |
|---|---|
| DIFFICULTY MODERATE | |
| HAZARD MODERATE | |
| MOUNTAIN HEIGHT 2480 M | |
| ELEVATION GAIN 780 M | |
| ROUND-TRIP DISTANCE APPROX. 5 KM | |
| ROUND-TRIP TIME 4–6 HOURS | |
| ADDITIONAL EQUIPMENT AVALANCHE GEAR MAY BE NECESSARY FOR THE UPPER SLOPES | |
| MAPS 82 J/14 SPRAY LAKE RESERVOIR, GEM TREK CANMORE | |

*This ascent, first brought to my attention by Bob Spirko, can vary from being relatively easy to very strenuous. The horizontal distance of the trip is short, but almost 800 m of elevation gain may have you gasping for breath when the snow is deep and unsupportive. Early-season ascents, and January outings, may not require snowshoes. The summit view is one of the best in the area.*

## DIRECTIONS

The trip starts at Spencer Creek (not identified on some maps), about 2.8 km south of Spurling Creek, on the Smith-Dorrien Highway (see photo A). Hike or snowshoe on the north side of the creek, heading east. There is a good summer trail here but you probably won't be able to follow it, because of the snow cover. About 10 minutes along, leave the creek and continue heading east and slightly north, through the trees.

The terrain eventually steepens and travel may become more strenuous. You'll soon (or later if you need to take additional time on the steep slope) arrive at a huge boulder field. Negotiating the field can be fun but also dangerous because of snow cover. If the field is snow-packed, it can be circumvented on the right side. Otherwise, weave your way through the boulders toward a prominent vertical rock face above. Either traverse below this face or swing around to the right and travel over it.

Above the rock face, continue going northeast, up along the ridge toward the summit. Routefinding is easy from here. Above treeline, avalanche gear might be a good precaution if the slopes are snow-loaded (**avalanche danger**). The summit block is steepest on the right side, so you'll want to swing around to the left to avoid it. Then, turn right and make your way easily to the summit at GR199469. The view of Mount Lougheed is fantastic from this viewpoint. Return the same way.

*ABOVE: [A] LITTLE LOUGHEED AND TWO OF THE FOUR DISTINCTIVE SUMMITS OF MOUNT LOUGHEED, AS SEEN FROM THE HIGHWAY. 1L=FIRST SUMMIT OF MOUNT LOUGHEED. LL=SUMMIT OF LITTLE LOUGHEED. TSL=TRUE SUMMIT OF MOUNT LOUGHEED. RIGHT: A LARGE CORNICE FAILS AND COMES CRASHING DOWN THE NORTH FACE OF MOUNT SPARROWHAWK.*

# 16 READ'S RIDGE

(MAP 6, PAGE 316)

| | |
|---|---|
| **DIFFICULTY** MODERATE | |
| **HAZARD** LOW | |
| **MOUNTAIN HEIGHT** 2353 M | |
| **ELEVATION GAIN** 646 M | |
| **ROUND-TRIP DISTANCE** 4 KM | |
| **ROUND-TRIP TIME** 3–5 HOURS | |
| **MAPS** 82 J/14 SPRAY LAKE RESERVOIR, GEM TREK CANMORE | |

*Read's Ridge is a relatively straightforward and safe ascent. The view from the top of Spray Lake and the surrounding mountains is fantastic. The trip is not terribly long or physically taxing unless you have to break trail by yourself all the way to the top. This is a "must-do" trip for the intermediate snowshoer. The route here is the same as that described by Gillean Daffern in her* Kananaskis Country Trail Guide, Volume 1.

## DIRECTIONS

Before parking at the Sparrowhawk day-use parking lot (locked during the winter but you can park at the side), it is a good idea to drive about 100 m south of the parking lot to check out the general direction of the ascent route from Sparrowhawk Creek (see photo A opposite). Once you start the ascent, views of the objective are practically non-existent until you are out of the trees. A quick look should make routefinding relatively simple.

From the parking lot, hike about 100 m south on the road, cross it and then snowshoe up the embankment on the north side of Sparrowhawk Creek. This is where the Sparrowhawk

Tarns Trail is, and you should look for a snowshoe trail to make life a little easier. The trail follows the north bank of Sparrowhawk Creek. As you move along, look up once in a while to check out the objective; it is east and slightly north of the route you are on and will sporadically pop into your field of vision. Once you leave the creek, you won't be able to see the ridge.

When the trail and creek start curving to the southeast, it's time for you to start curving to the northeast. Hopefully a previous party has done so already. Routefinding your way to Read's Ridge is not difficult, but the objective is not visible until you actually arrive there. Just go up and northeast, aiming for GR196444. There are several ribs at which you may lose a little elevation before resuming the uphill grind. However, if you start losing a large amount of elevation, you have probably gone too far north and are now heading down into Forbes Creek. Veer sharply to the right and up if this happens.

At GR196444, 2220 m, you are officially on Read's Ridge and

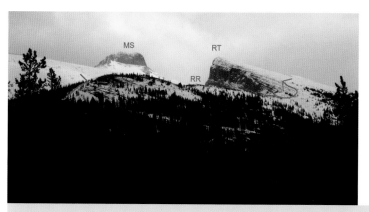

[A] A CLOSE-UP LOOK AT READ'S RIDGE AND TOWER, AS SEEN FROM THE HIGHWAY. RR=READ'S RIDGE. RT=READ'S TOWER. MS=MOUNT SPARROWHAWK.

can now follow it southeast to its highpoint. Undoubtedly the magnificent view of Read's Tower, with Mount Sparrowhawk perched high above to the left, will be a source of satisfaction, as you make your way up. The summit lies at GR201442, 2353 m. The prominent peaks towering above Spray Lake to the west are Mount Nestor and Old Goat Mountain.

Return the same way if you are done for the day. If the more serious objective of Read's Tower is in your plans, continue on to the next trip, no. 17, Read's Tower.

READ'S TOWER IS TO THE RIGHT.
MOUNT SPARROWHAWK IS AT THE DISTANT LEFT.

# 17 READ'S TOWER

(MAP 6, PAGE 316)

| | |
|---|---|
| DIFFICULTY | DIFFICULT |
| HAZARD | HIGH |
| MOUNTAIN HEIGHT | 2627 M |
| ELEVATION GAIN | 920 M |
| ROUND-TRIP DISTANCE | 5.5 KM |
| ROUND-TRIP TIME | 5–8 HOURS |
| ADDITIONAL EQUIPMENT | AVALANCHE GEAR, CRAMPONS, ICE AXE |
| MAPS | 82 J/14 SPRAY LAKE RESERVOIR, GEM TREK KANANASKIS LAKES |

*Read's Tower is about 275 vertical m higher than Read's Ridge and, needless to say, sports a far more comprehensive view of this beautiful area. In certain conditions the ascent will be nothing more than an innocuous, steep scree hike. At other times, it can involve steep snow or ice with avalanche potential. That being the case, crampons, an ice axe and stable snow conditions will all be needed on this trip.*

## DIRECTIONS

Follow the directions up to Read's Ridge from the previous trip description (see page 146). With the right conditions it is possible to reach the summit from Read's Ridge with snowshoes on, but most people will choose to go on foot, with or without crampons. Crampons are definitely recommended when the snow is too hard to step-kick into. Leave your snowshoes on Read's Ridge. From the ridge, the route up Read's Tower is very obvious. Lose a small amount of elevation and then follow the ridge east to the summit. The slope is steepest at the beginning and then eases up a little for the final 100 vertical m. Still, the grade falls within that magical range of 25°–60°, where avalanches are possible – be cautious and alert (**avalanche danger**).

As long as you don't step onto the cornice on the left and plummet to a premature death, the best route follows the left edge of the tower. From the top, plenty of familiar and distinctive peaks are visible to the north and south.

Return the same way. **Do not** try to take a direct route down to Sparrowhawk Creek. As well as being a huge avalanche slope, the lower sections of such a route are lined with cliff-bands.

SASTRUGI (SNOW ERODED INTO RIDGES AND GROOVES BY WIND) NEAR THE SUMMIT OF READ'S TOWER.

# 18 RED RIDGE

(MAP 6, PAGE 316)

| | |
|---|---|
| **DIFFICULTY** MODERATE—DIFFICULT | |
| **HAZARD** MODERATE—HIGH | |
| **MOUNTAIN HEIGHT** 2645 M | |
| **ELEVATION GAIN** 930 M | |
| **ROUND-TRIP DISTANCE** 8—10 KM | |
| **ROUND-TRIP TIME** 6—8 HOURS | |
| **ADDITIONAL EQUIPMENT** AVALANCHE GEAR, ICE AXE | |
| **MAPS** 82 J/14 SPRAY LAKE RESERVOIR, GEM TREK CANMORE | |

*Depending on snow conditions, an ascent of Red Ridge can range from a steep hike and easy scramble to a near-mountaineering experience. A late-April snowstorm in 2010 ensured our early-May ascent was closer to the latter. There are two routes to the ridge, the direct one being shorter and steeper than the northwest-ridge route. In general the trip is very similar to that ascending Red Ridge's neighbour to the north, Read's Tower. However, the scenery along Red Ridge is significantly better.*

## DIRECTIONS

### Direct route

This is the same route as that described in Gillean Daffern's *Kananaskis Country Trail Guide, Volume 1*. Park at the Spray Lakes day-use area. Drive about 100 m south, past the parking area, if you want to get a look at the general ascent route and condition of the upper slopes. From the parking area, hike a short distance south to an unnamed creek. The summer trail runs parallel to the creek on its north side. In the likely event that the official trail is snow-covered and therefore difficult to find and follow, simply follow the creek as it goes east and slightly south. About 800 m from the road (GR186428), turn left and start going east and slightly north uphill. The terrain is steep in places but not relentlessly so. Still, this part of the trip will definitely give "the old ticker" a good workout.

Aim for the start of the ridge at GR1942429. Expect this section to take at least 1.5 hours and possibly more if the trail-breaking is strenuous. The usual advice to persevere is very fitting here, as the magnificent scenery on the upper ridge is well worth any amount of physical effort to get there.

### Northwest ridge route

This route is longer than the direct one, but it goes up at a gentler grade. It will probably be the route of choice for most parties. Park at the Sparrowhawk day-use parking lot or about 300 m farther south, depending on where it is the safest to park. Hike the 300 m southward if you didn't drive it, and then turn east into the forest. Snowshoe or hike about 800 m east toward the start of the NW ridge. You'll know you've gone too far east if you start dropping down into Sparrowhawk Creek. Around GR188438, turn southeast and head up the wide ridge, aiming for GR194429. Allow two hours to reach GR194429 from the road; more if the trail-breaking is difficult.

### To the summit (for both routes)

Once on the ridge, the direction of travel requires no explanation. Simply go southeast until you arrive at the summit at GR211419. However, I don't mean to imply that the ascent will be easy. The ridge has several ups and downs, and the summit is still quite a distance away. Side-sloping in places is certainly feasible, but those who follow the ridge will be rewarded with some stunning scenery on the steep north face. Cornices can overhang the ridge

TYPICAL CORNICES ON THE RED RIDGE.

by huge distances: **be cautious**. Snowshoes and an ice axe may or may not be required.

The crux of the ridge occurs about halfway up, at GR11 620371E 5642264N, 2430 m (see photo A, next page). Here, the ridge suddenly drops off. It is recognizable by the terrain ahead (see photo A). Descend a short, steep slope on the left side of the ridge and continue up the other side. This section is also steep and can be an avalanche concern (**avalanche danger**). Go over to the right side to find gentler terrain. Ascend this slope and then immediately regain the ridge.

The most scenic part of the trip remains as you follow the ridge to the summit, enjoying fantastic cornice scenery along the way. The wonderful forms of mounts Sparrowhawk, Bogart and Buller are also there to keep you company. The summit view is excellent in all directions. The challenging-looking peak that shares a col with Red Ridge to the south is "North Buller Pass Peak" (see page 158). After taking it all in, return the same way. Alternative descent routes are possible, but they present significant avalanche concern. It's best to play it safe here.

ABOVE: [A] C=THE CRUX; GO DOWN THE LEFT (NORTH) SIDE OF THE RIDGE HERE. AS=AVALANCHE SLOPES; THE TERRAIN HERE IS MUCH STEEPER THAN IT APPEARS. E=EASIER ROUTE. BELOW: TYPICAL SCENERY ON THE WAY UP RED RIDGE.

# 19 NORTH RIDGE OF MOUNT BULLER

(MAP 6, PAGE 316)

**DIFFICULTY** MODERATE, STEEP SECTIONS THROUGH THE TREES

**HAZARD** LOW TO THE RIDGE, MODERATE TO THE HIGHEST POINT

**RIDGE HEIGHT** 2260 M, HIGHEST POINT 2350 M

**ELEVATION GAIN** RIDGE 500 M, HIGHEST POINT 600 M

**ROUND-TRIP DISTANCE** 3.5–5 KM

**ROUND-TRIP TIME** 3–5 HOURS

**ADDITIONAL EQUIPMENT** AVALANCHE GEAR; CRAMPONS AND ICE AXE FOR THE HIGHEST POINT

**MAPS** 82 J/14 SPRAY LAKE RESERVOIR, GEM TREK KANANASKIS LAKES

*If the avalanche risk in the area is high, this trip offers a relatively safe ascent to a good viewpoint. Continuing to the highest point requires avalanche gear and possibly other gear. Wait for a clear day and go with a group to share the very strenuous trail-breaking duties.*

## DIRECTIONS

Park at the side of Highway 742 about 2 km south of the Spray Lakes parking lot. The treed ridge is visible as you approach the parking area. Although it is possible to avoid bushwhacking by following an open drainage south of the suggested parking area, that route will expose you to dangerous avalanche slopes.

Therefore, an ascent through the trees is recommended, though it is tedious and not scenic. Head into the trees, and make for the southeast. When the terrain starts to steepen, it is best to find one of several wide ribs between depressions to ascend, though any route will do. If anything, trend slightly to the right as you go up. Patience and perseverance are required: the slope is longer than you may think. If the snow is deep and unconsolidated, expect to take 1.5–2 gruelling hours to get to the ridge.

Upon reaching the wide treed ridge, turn right (south) toward the open north ridge of Mount Buller, at GR191409, 2260 m. The view is quite respectable for a relatively low elevation. If you are done for the day, return the same way. Thankfully, the descent should be very easy and very fast. Expect to take only 45 minutes or less to get back to the road.

### Extension up the North Ridge of Buller

Continuing the trip up the north ridge of Buller is a very short and worthwhile extension if time and conditions permit. Although staying on the crest of the ridge will minimize avalanche risk, it may be corniced and therefore dangerous. Use discretion.

Lose a little elevation to a small col and then continue south up the ridge. Crampons and an ice axe may be more appropriate than snowshoes here. Stop at the flat area at GR188403, 2350 m. Travelling beyond this point is not advised because of increased avalanche risk and exposure on both sides of the ridge. The views are not much different from what you experienced atop the north ridge, but looking along the south ridge that continues to Mount Buller is very interesting (and tempting!). Return the same way.

DESCENDING TO THE LOW POINT, BEFORE
CONTINUING SOUTH, UP THE RIDGE.

# 20 "NORTH BULLER PASS PEAK"

(MAP 6, PAGE 316)

| | |
|---|---|
| DIFFICULTY | MODERATE TO NORTH BULLER PASS, DIFFICULT TO THE PEAK |
| HAZARD | HIGH |
| MOUNTAIN HEIGHT | 2755 M |
| ELEVATION GAIN | 940 M |
| ROUND-TRIP DISTANCE | 14–16 KM |
| ROUND-TRIP TIME | 8–10 HOURS |
| ADDITIONAL EQUIPMENT | AVALANCHE GEAR, CRAMPONS, ICE AXE |
| MAPS | 82 J/14 SPRAY LAKE RESERVOIR, GEM TREK CANMORE |

*The valley south of Mount Buller is a terrific snowshoeing and skiing destination. Several highpoints and unnamed summits offer excellent views. North Buller Pass and the unofficial peak to the north (also called "Red Peak" in Gillean Daffern's new* Kananaskis Country Trail Guide, Vol. 1) *are especially appealing because of their high elevation. Access to the pass and peak is straightforward but long. Be prepared for a very full and physically demanding day.*

## DIRECTIONS

Park at the Buller Mountain day-use parking lot, near the south end of Spray Lake. Cross the road and find the signed Buller Pass trailhead. This trail is well used throughout the winter. Unfortunately, it is fairly narrow in many sections, making it difficult to have separate trails for skiers and hikers/snowshoers. Do your best to avoid the ski trail, if it exists, though trekking a common trail will be necessary for several long stretches. The trail soon descends to Buller Creek, crosses to the north side of it and then continues up the valley, high above the creek. A couple of kilometres after the first creek crossing, cross the creek again on a log bridge and then work your way uphill to the right, following several switchbacks if they are visible. This takes you to the upper valley, where the creek soon forks at around GR190381, 1800 m. Hopefully, travel up to this point has been easy because of the well-used trail. If not, you may have to downgrade your objective for the day, as there is still some distance and much elevation to cover.

At GR190381 take the left fork toward North Buller Pass (the right fork goes to Buller Pass). Again, the trail here may be very prominent or may be non-existent, depending on conditions. The goal is to work your way into the valley immediately southeast of Mount Buller. You can use the long and interesting east ridge of Mount Buller as a guideline. Although the summer trail crosses over to the north side of the creek, travelling right over the creek is easier and quite scenic. Be aware, however, that short sections of the creek could be terrain traps (**avalanche danger**). Move quickly through these sections and spread out. If avalanches are a concern, you may want to gain elevation on the north side of the creek and go through the trees.

When you arrive at a small frozen waterfall, go up and around its left side and then continue up the wide, open valley. This beautiful valley is a worthwhile destination in itself. North Buller Pass is the obvious low col at the end of the valley (see photo A on next page). Go to the end of the valley and make your way up to the col, taking the least steep route. This is serious avalanche terrain and needs to be treated with caution (**avalanche danger**).

The view from the pass is excellent toward the north and south peaks of Mount Kidd and Ribbon Lake, and you certainly experience a sense of accomplishment having made it this far. Return the same way if you have had enough or if dangerous snow conditions preclude continuing to North Buller Pass Peak.

If conditions are good and you feel comfortable on steeper and more dangerous terrain than that required in getting to the pass, continuing on to North Buller Pass Peak is a very rewarding extension. The summit of North Buller is not visible from the pass, because it lies to the north. Now comes the trickiest and potentially the most dangerous part of the trip. You have to get around the immediate summit to the north and gain the ridge that connects this summit to the summit of North Buller Pass Peak. More than likely you will trade your snowshoes here for crampons and ice axe. Take the shoes with you, however, just in case the connecting ridge is plastered in deep, unconsolidated snow.

[A] IN THE NORTH BULLER PASS VALLEY, SOUTHEAST OF MOUNT BULLER. C=COL.

[B] BACK ON THE RIDGE AFTER CIRCUMVENTING THE UNNAMED SUMMIT. NBPP=THE SUMMIT. MB=MOUNT BOGART.

NBPP

MB

There are two routes to get over to the ridge. The feasibility of each depends on the amount of snow and the snow conditions. Be prepared to call it a day at the col, if conditions are unsafe.

### Route 1

Ascend the ridge north toward the unnamed summit (**avalanche danger**). Just before reaching the rock-band, swing out to the right onto the east-facing slopes. These slopes are steep and avalanche-prone, but they may be windblasted and free of snow. If they are snow-covered, crampons and an ice axe are mandatory. Side-slope over to the ridge on the north side of the unnamed summit. The summit of North Buller finally comes into view along the way (see photo B). Once you are on the ridge, it's an easy walk to the summit, with one minor detour on the left side to circumvent a drop-off.

### Route 2

From the col, descend steep avalanche slopes to the east, provided there is not a cornice preventing you from even getting onto these slopes (**avalanche danger**). Again, this is crampons-and-ice-axe terrain, not snowshoe terrain. Lose elevation onto gentler slopes and then swing around to the left (north) to gain the col south of North Buller Pass Peak. Follow the ridge north to the summit, with one minor detour on the left side to circumvent a drop-off.

### The summit (both routes)

The summit view is outstanding. Several of Kananaskis's highest are close by – Bogart, Sparrowhawk, Galatea, Old Goat – and Spray Lake stretches out to the northwest. Red Ridge lies immediately to the north, and the long ridge to Bogart to the east. Unfortunately, continuing along either of these lines requires some serious climbing gear and technique. Return the same way you came in.

# 21 RUMMEL LAKE

(MAP 6, PAGE 316)

| | |
|---|---|
| **DIFFICULTY** EASY | |
| **HAZARD** LOW | |
| **LAKE HEIGHT** 2217 M | |
| **ELEVATION GAIN** 350 M | |
| **ROUND TRIP DISTANCE** 10 KM | |
| **ROUND TRIP TIME** 5–7 HOURS | |
| **MAPS** 82 J/14 SPRAY LAKE RESERVOIR, GEM TREK CANMORE, GEM TREK KANANASKIS LAKES | |

*Rummel Lake is a decent destination for snowshoers and skiers. However, the minor summit northwest of the lake offers an excellent view and is a far more worthwhile objective. The price may be several kilometres of strenuous uphill trail-breaking. Take a companion (or four) to ease the strain! There is a winter backcountry campground at Rummel Lake for those who wish to make this a multi-day trip. A permit to camp is required and can be picked up at any park information centre.*

## DIRECTIONS

There are two approaches for the Rummel Lake trip and for "Rummel Ridge" as well (see page 166): a summer trail that starts at the Engadine Lodge turnoff; or a cutline a few hundred metres south of the turnoff. The cutline is more direct, but you may have to break trail for its length. On the other hand, the summer trail is well used in winter and therefore often packed down. Most will choose the ease of the summer trail as opposed to the shorter length of the cutline. The summer trail route is described below.

Park on the east side of the Smith-Dorrien Highway, opposite the turnoff to Engadine Lodge, about 7.5 km north of the Chester Lake parking lot. The trail quickly ascends into the trees and then parallels the highway heading SSE. After several hundred metres, it turns back on itself, now heading NE. There is a small shortcut before the turn that you may be able to take if the trail is broken. Soon the terrain opens up a little, revealing pleasant views to the west. If your goal is Rummel Ridge, it will soon be visible to the SE as a very plain-looking, treed hump (see photo A opposite). Take note to avoid ascending the wrong peak.

The trail then swings around and heads in a southeasterly direction. Eventually it goes back into the trees, following a ridge high above Rummel Creek. Stay on this ridge as it starts to curve around to the east toward Rummel Lake, losing a little elevation along the way. Cross to the north side of Rummel Creek around GR192324 and follow the creek or perhaps a well-packed snowshoe trail east of the west side of Rummel Lake. Return the same way or extend your day by visiting the beautiful valley northeast of the lake. Rummel Ridge (see page 166) is also a possible trip extension.

### Extension to the Upper Valley

To visit the upper valley between Mount Galatea and The Tower, snowshoe to the northeast end of Rummel Lake and then turn north. About 300 m of uphill snowshoeing takes you above treeline and out into the open. Turn east and continue up the valley for as long as you wish. Return the same way.

[A] THE FIRST DECENT VIEW OF RUMMEL RIDGE AND THE TOWER.
RR=RUMMEL RIDGE. SW=SOUTHWEST RIDGE OF THE TOWER.
TT=SUMMIT OF THE TOWER.

# 22 "RUMMEL RIDGE"

(MAP 6, PAGE 316)

| | |
|---|---|
| DIFFICULTY MODERATE | |
| HAZARD MODERATE | |
| RIDGE HEIGHT 2459 M | |
| ELEVATION GAIN 800 M | |
| ROUND-TRIP DISTANCE 8.5 KM | |
| ROUND-TRIP TIME 6–9 HOURS | |
| ADDITIONAL EQUIPMENT AVALANCHE GEAR | |
| MAPS 82 J/14 SPRAY LAKE RESERVOIR, GEM TREK CANMORE, GEM TREK KANANASKIS LAKES | |

*This highpoint above Rummel Lake provides an excellent view and is likely to become a very popular extension or alternative to the already popular Rummel Lake trip. If the ridge is your only destination, it is not necessary to go all the way to Rummel Lake. The goal is to follow the summer trail or the cutline to a point south of Rummel Ridge and then go north to the summit.*

## DIRECTIONS

Follow the directions for Rummel Lake (see page 163) until you arrive at the ridge that parallels Rummel Creek. Look for the cutline crossing the trail somewhere around GR183326. Turn left onto the cutline and follow it down to Rummel Creek and then up the other side. Stay on the cutline until it starts to descend to Rummel Lake. At this point, the most direct route takes a sharp turn north (left) and heads straight for the summit. You will be in the trees, so routefinding may be necessary. If you are using GPS, you'll find that the summit lies at GR190335. You can

trend farther east to more open areas, but that may put you on avalanche slopes (**avalanche danger**). Most of the hazardous terrain is avoidable with good routefinding. As always, packing avalanche gear is a wise precaution.

The view in all directions is excellent. Of course, it is limited to the east, but the impressive form of the ranges' tallest peak, Mount Galatea, should impress you. Return the same way or extend your trip to ascend a short section of the southwest ridge of The Tower.

### Extension up the southwest ridge of The Tower

If you want a slightly higher and better viewpoint, it is possible to ascend a short section of the southwest ridge of The Tower, northeast of Rummel Ridge. This continuation of the trip requires discretion and good judgment, as the **avalanche danger** increases here. Simply descend to the col between the ridge and

MOUNT GALATEA.

The Tower and then proceed up the southwest slopes. Follow the ridge north for as far as your ability and comfort level dictate. Don't get any grandiose ideas about making the summit of The Tower via this route; the ridge eventually comes to a drop-off that will repel all those who can't rappel. (Finally, I get to use "repel" and "rappel" in the same sentence!)

# 23 MOUNT FORTUNE AND FORTULENT PEAK

(MAP 6, PAGE 316)

DIFFICULTY MODERATE TO FORTUNE, DIFFICULT TO FORTULENT

HAZARD MODERATE TO FORTUNE, HIGH TO FORTULENT

MOUNTAIN HEIGHTS FORTUNE 2350 M, FORTULENT 2520 M

ELEVATION GAIN FORTUNE 675 M, ADD 200 M FOR FORTULENT

ROUND-TRIP DISTANCE APPROX. 12 KM FOR FORTUNE, 16–18 KM FOR FORTULENT AND BEYOND

ROUND-TRIP TIME 5–9 HOURS

ADDITIONAL EQUIPMENT AVALANCHE GEAR, CRAMPONS, AND ICE AXE FOR FORTULENT

MAPS 82 J/14 SPRAY LAKE RESERVOIR, GEM TREK CANMORE

*This is one of the best snowshoe trips in the area. The scenery around the southwest end of Spray Lake is excellent, and even a short trip onto the lake is a worthwhile excursion on a clear day. The summit of Fortune offers an outstanding view, and the summit of Fortulent an even better one. Again, wait for a clear day to best experience these wonderful panoramas.*

## DIRECTIONS

Driving south on Highway 742, turn right at the Engadine Lodge turnoff and follow the road to the Shark Mountain parking lot.

The first order of business is to make it down to Spray Lake. This can be accomplished by following a maze of ski trails. Be considerate of skiers on these groomed trails and stay off to the side. You need to locate the Watridge Lake trailhead, which is at the northwest end of the parking lot and descends immediately for a few metres and then heads west in a straight line. Follow this trail for about 500 m. Turn right at the first intersection, ascend a short hill and then turn left onto a trail that immediately descends toward Spray Lake. Follow this down, and when it curves around to the west (left), turn right, into the trees, and make your way to the lake in a matter of minutes.

At the shore of Spray Lake, Mount Fortune is immediately visible across the lake, appearing as a low, rounded hump. Point yourself in that direction (NNW) and off you go. There are several small islands in the middle of the lake, so don't be alarmed when you start going slightly uphill. The southwest end of Spray Lake can be an interesting and fulfilling adventure in itself, depending on the weather conditions and the state of the ice. Windblown sections of the lake surface may be free of snow, revealing huge cracks in the ice, as well as air bubbles and other fascinating phenomena. In other parts, huge slabs of ice may have collided with each other as they expanded when freezing, pushing each other up in a process similar to that of mountain building. Of course, the lake may be covered in deep snow with no exposed ice at all, in which case you'll probably just hurry across. In addition to the ice scenery, the middle of the lake affords a terrific view of the surrounding mountains. Morrison, Turner and Cone may be particularly eye-catching, especially on a clear day.

The upper ridge of Mount Fortune can be reached from either the southeast or southwest side of the mountain. The southeast is a little steeper and so the southwest is the recommended route. As you cross the lake, aim for the clear area beneath the rock of the south face (see photo). Gain West Side Trail, very near the shoreline, and follow it west for several hundred metres. While there are open slopes to the ridge immediately west of the interesting rock ribs of the south face, it is best to continue a little farther west and ascend through the trees. This route is a little less steep than the slopes and definitely less prone to avalanche. If the slopes are snow-free, however, ascend closer to the ribs for some interesting scenery. From West Side Trail, turn right (north) and ascend slopes to gain the wide ridge. Upon reaching the ridge, follow it north on easy terrain to the summit of Mount Fortune (GR117390).

For a mountain that rises only to 2350 metres, Fortune's summit view is terrific. Cone Mountain immediately to the west is guaranteed to impress, as are Old Goat and Nestor on the other

THE SOUTH SIDE OF MOUNT FORTUNE, AS SEEN FROM THE SOUTHWEST END OF SPRAY LAKE. AN UNUSUAL LACK OF SNOW FOR FEBRUARY. S=SUMMIT OF MOUNT FORTUNE.

side. For an even better view, continue the trip north to Fortulent Peak. Return the same way if Fortulent in not an option. Alternatively, if the snow is stable, it is also possible to descend the huge gully on the west side of the peak. If you choose this route, descend from the summit the way you came for several hundred metres and then head right (west) down into the gully. With stable conditions and good snow, this gully can be glissaded in no time. It is steep near the top, however, and good ice-axe technique will be required. At the bottom of the gully keep going south toward West Side Trail and Spray Lake.

### On to Fortulent Peak

The ascent to Fortulent Peak will require stable snow conditions or, better yet, no snow at all on the main slope (not common, but it did occur on our February 2009 trip). On a clear day the visual rewards of this extension are amazing. The route is very obvious (see photo opposite).

Descend to the col between Fortune and Fortulent and ascend the south ridge of Fortulent (**avalanche danger**). Stay in the middle of the ridge to avoid starting an avalanche down either side. The terrain gets a little steeper toward the top and requires a few scrambling moves around the left side. If these slopes are completely plastered, you may prefer crampons and an ice axe to snowshoes. After the scrambling, the summit is only a short walk away (GR111397). While the view to the east, south and west is similar to that on Fortune's top, the view to the north is considerably better on Fortulent: the highlight of this view is the long ridge to the summit of Turbulent Mountain.

Fortulent has a twin peak several hundred metres to the north. The traverse to the second peak is easy and short and gives you a good view of the east face of the peak. Be aware of potentially big cornices. Continuing north along the scenic ridge from the twin-peak summit is also an easy affair. It is possible

S=SUMMIT OF FORTULENT PEAK. TP=TWIN PEAK OF FORTULENT.

to reach a significant summit about 1.5 km farther, though this will make for a fairly long day and return trip. Most will probably be content to go to the next highpoint north of Fortulent's twin peak and then turn around (GR111404, 2500 m). There's another great view of the east face of Fortulent on the way there – make sure you turn around to see it!

Return the same way when you've had enough or run out of time. See the Mount Fortune directions above for an alternative descent route from the summit of Fortune.

ABOVE: ENJOYING THE FINE VIEW FROM THE TWIN PEAK OF FORTULENT. BELOW: RETURNING TO FORTULENT'S TWIN PEAK AFTER A SHORT CONTINUATION NORTH.

# 24 SMUTS PASS

(MAP 6, PAGE 316)

| | |
|---|---|
| DIFFICULTY | DIFFICULT |
| HAZARD | HIGH |
| PASS HEIGHT | 2332 M |
| ELEVATION GAIN | 400 M |
| ROUND-TRIP DISTANCE | 10–12 KM |
| ROUND-TRIP TIME | 6–8 HOURS |
| ADDITIONAL EQUIPMENT | AVALANCHE GEAR |
| MAPS | 82 J/14 SPRAY LAKES RESERVOIR, GEM TREK KANANASKIS LAKES |

*Smuts Pass is another popular destination for backcountry skiers. Routefinding can be a little tricky at the beginning of this trip, especially if you are the first to break trail into the Commonwealth Creek valley. Those with mountaineering experience may wish to tack on the extension to this trip, an ascent of unofficially named "Smutwood Peak."*

## DIRECTIONS

Drive 2.2 km south of the Engadine Lodge turnoff and park on the west side of the road, around GR176312. Look west, across the flats of Smuts Creek, for a small gap in the trees (see the photo for "Commonwealth Ridge" on page 187). Snowshoe across the flats and go through the gap. The path trends slightly right before arriving at a "No camping/fires" sign. This is a very popular area so expect there to be a multitude of trails. As you approach the sign, go slightly left into the trees and head southwest. You'll soon arrive at another popular trail that runs north–south. The terrain opens up a little and the route should become more obvious.

At this point you should look for a cutline running southwest, south of Commonwealth Creek. To find it, follow the trail going toward the distinctive form of The Fist (see photo A below). The trail soon swings around to the left and then arrives at an open area, where it forks (GR168304). This fork is not always obvious. The right fork leads to Smuts Pass, the left to Commonwealth Lake – take the right.

The route then follows the south hillside above Commonwealth Creek. The summer trail stays on the north side of the creek. At one point you will cross over another creek that originates from Commonwealth Lake, although snow cover may hide it. Stay above Commonwealth Creek, eventually arriving at the scenic valley. Here the trail will probably trend right and cross

[A] A CLOSE-UP LOOK AT THE DISTINCTIVE FORM OF THE FIST. YOU'LL WANT TO BE LEFT (SOUTH) OF THE FIST.

over to the north side of the creek. Regardless, the route is obvious once you are out in the open.

Travel southwest on the north side of the wide valley, with the impressive east face of Mount Birdwood ever present ahead of you. You will more than likely be paralleling a ski track. Again, remember to make a separate snowshoe track where possible.

On the way to the head of the valley, you'll pass by The Fist and a few avalanche slopes. Avalanche fatalities have occurred in this area, so be wary (**avalanche danger**). Past these slopes, the trail continues up the valley toward a significant treed hill ahead. In summer the trail goes up this hill and then descends back down to the valley. The easiest route in winter, provided the creek is significantly covered, is to stay at the bottom of the valley and follow Commonwealth Creek around the left side of the hill.

SNOWSHOEING UP COMMONWEALTH CREEK VALLEY. MOUNT SMUTS IS TO THE RIGHT AND SMUTS PASS IS THE OBVIOUS LOW COL.

Once around the hill, there are a couple of routes to Smuts Pass. The easiest and most scenic (but also the most dangerous) ascends open slopes at the end of the valley, under the east face of Mount Birdwood. A much safer, but potentially very strenuous, route follows a small drainage through the trees east of the dangerous route.

### Dangerous but scenic route

Simply snowshoe to the end of the valley and then turn right, going up slopes of varying degrees (mostly in the **avalanche danger** range). Specific route options are numerous, but you may want to trend right as you go up, making your way onto less steep terrain. Smuts Pass is 350 vertical m above you.

### Safer route

Once you are around the hill, head into the trees to the right and look for a drainage to follow. You may or may not be able to locate this drainage, but as long as you are going west you should be okay. As mentioned previously, even if a trail has been broken, this part of the trip could be very physically taxing. Persevere up the lower (and steepest) slopes knowing that easier terrain sits above.

Near treeline the angle eases. When the terrain opens up, so do several potential routes to Smuts Pass. The least steep route stays right and traverses slopes beneath the south face of Mount Smuts. Even so, there is definitely some **avalanche danger** here and all precautions should be taken. Work up to the obvious col between Mount Birdwood and Mount Smuts. The view at the pass is excellent in good weather. Consider continuing on to "Smutwood Peak" (next trip) or return the same way.

A GREAT VIEW OF MOUNT SMUTS IS REVEALED WHEN
NEARING SMUTS PASS. THE SCRAMBLE ROUTE FOLLOWS
THE SNOWY SOUTH RIDGE AT THE RIGHT.

# 25 "SMUTWOOD PEAK"

(MAP 6, PAGE 316)

DIFFICULTY DIFFICULT, MOUNTAINEERING

HAZARD HIGH

MOUNTAIN HEIGHT 2690 M

ELEVATION GAIN 800 M

ROUND-TRIP DISTANCE 14–16 KM

ROUND-TRIP TIME 9–12 HOURS

ADDITIONAL EQUIPMENT AVALANCHE GEAR,
CRAMPONS, ICE AXE

MAPS 82 J/14 SPRAY LAKES RESERVOIR,
GEM TREK KANANASKIS LAKES

*If you've made it to Smuts Pass and want phenomenal views of Mount Birdwood, Mount Smuts and an array of beautiful peaks to the west, the unofficially named "Smutwood Peak" is an excellent destination. It is also a very long and difficult trip, requiring travellers to make good assessments of snow conditions. Stay away from this trip if the avalanche hazard is "considerable" or higher. Proficiency with crampons and an ice axe and being comfortable on steep, exposed terrain are requirements of this extension to Smuts Pass. This trip definitely has a mountaineering feel to it.*

## DIRECTIONS

Follow the previous directions to Smuts Pass (page 175). From the pass, take a look to the west to assess conditions and the best route to the col between Smutwood and Birdwood (see photo A opposite). Either side-slope to the col or drop down to the lake and then work your work up to the col from there. If the snow is stable, side-sloping is a relatively safe option, though these slopes can be threatened from above by large cornices. Pick the least steep route.

At the col, trade your snowshoes for crampons and an ice axe and follow the southeast ridge toward the false summit. Steep sections are thankfully short-lived, but cornices overhanging the east face can be significant – stay away from the edge. A rock-band interrupts progress but you can avoid it by dropping down to the left for a short distance and then going around the band. Return to the ridge right away. The terrain gets a little more serious near the false summit. To avoid travelling on potential avalanche slopes, stay on the edge of the ridge, again being mindful of cornices.

If getting to the false summit (GR129285, 2590 m) has been a challenge, you will probably want to call it a day, enjoy the magnificent view and return the same way you came. The traverse to the true summit is steeper and more exposed and will put you on slopes with high avalanche potential. The false summit is a more

[A] Smutwood Peak and variations, as seen from Smuts Pass. Slope grades are very deceiving here – "Sepia Ridge" is far more serious than it appears. FS=false summit. TS=true summit. SR=Sepia Ridge. LR=long route up Sepia Ridge. DR=direct route.

than worthwhile stopping point and only a small portion of a full 360° panorama is missing.

If snow conditions are good and you are confident about the traverse to the true summit, simply continue north along the ridge, at first losing a little elevation. The initial section of the ascent is easy but it gets much steeper and exposed near the top. The cornice near the summit may force you out onto the west slopes, which can be very avalanche-prone (**severe avalanche danger**). Err on the side of caution here and retreat if necessary.

Enjoy a terrific summit panorama in all directions before returning the same way. **Do not** continue west to the next highpoint. It is slightly lower than the true summit, very exposed and dangerous to get to.

*ABOVE: REACHING THE BIRDWOOD–SMUTWOOD COL, WITH MOUNT SMUTS BEHIND. RIGHT: CHALLENGING TERRAIN ON THE WAY TO THE FALSE SUMMIT.*

"SEPIA RIDGE"

(MAP 6, PAGE 316)

| | |
|---|---|
| DIFFICULTY | DIFFICULT, MOUNTAINEERING |
| HAZARD | HIGH |
| MOUNTAIN HEIGHT | 2570 M |
| ELEVATION GAIN | 680 M |
| ROUND-TRIP DISTANCE | 13–15 KM |
| ROUND-TRIP TIME | 8–12 HOURS |
| ADDITIONAL EQUIPMENT | AVALANCHE GEAR, CRAMPONS, ICE AXE |
| MAPS | 82 J/14 SPRAY LAKES RESERVOIR, GEM TREK KANANASKIS LAKES |

The summit of "Sepia Ridge" (as named by Calvin Damen in 2007) offers what may be the best view of one of the most beautiful mountains in the Canadian Rockies – Mount Birdwood. The summit of Sepia is directly in line with Birdwood's striking north ridge. Since both the east and west faces of the mountain are extremely steep, the profile of Birdwood from Sepia resembles a huge fang. As well, at either end of daylight, one side of the peak will be completely in shadow, the other fully illuminated by the sun. This view on a clear winter day is guaranteed to leave anyone breathless.

However, reaching the top of the ridge is far from easy. The upper slopes tilt to about 45°, pushing this route well into the category of mountaineering. As expected, very stable snow conditions, crampons and an ice axe are mandatory for this ascent. To ensure the best snow stability, only attempt this ascent late in the season.

## DIRECTIONS

There are two routes to the ascent slope of Sepia (see photo A on page 181). The direct route is steeper and may have more avalanche danger. The longer but safer route around the south end of the Lower Birdwood Lake is therefore recommended.

### Direct route

From Smuts Pass, head northwest down to Lower Birdwood Lake. Go around the north side of the lake and gain the upper tier, where Upper Birdwood Lake sits. The terrain going up to the ridge is quite steep and will require stable snow conditions (**avalanche danger**). Crampons and an ice axe may also be necessary.

### Longer but safer route

From Smuts Pass, head southwest down to the south end of Lower Birdwood Lake. Go around the south side of the lake and look for the safest (least steep) route to ascend to the upper tier. Gain the upper tier and snowshoe NNW to the start of Sepia's ascent slope.

### To the summit (for both routes)

Follow the ridge in a NNW direction up toward the summit (the highpoint in the centre of the ridge that connects Smutwood to Smuts). Leave your snowshoes when the grade starts to increase. The upper slopes are dangerously steep (**severe avalanche danger**). **Do not** ascend these slopes without a careful assessment of snow conditions and the requisite skills for steep snow and ice. Back down if travel gets dicey. After thoroughly absorbing the jaw-dropping view of Birdwood, return the same way you came in.

# 27 "COMMONWEALTH RIDGE"

(MAP 6, PAGE 316)

DIFFICULTY MODERATE TO THE NORTH SUMMIT, DIFFICULT TO CENTRE AND TRUE SUMMITS

HAZARD LOW TO NORTH SUMMIT, HIGH TO CENTRE AND TRUE SUMMITS

MOUNTAIN HEIGHT NORTH SUMMIT 2368 M, CENTRE SUMMIT 2550 M, TRUE SUMMIT 2561 M

ELEVATION GAIN NORTH SUMMIT 530 M, CENTRE SUMMIT 710 M, TRUE SUMMIT 750 M (INCLUDES A SMALL ELEVATION LOSS)

ROUND-TRIP DISTANCE 14–16 KM

ROUND-TRIP TIME 4–7 HOURS

ADDITIONAL EQUIPMENT NOTHING FOR NORTH SUMMIT, CRAMPONS AND ICE AXE FOR CENTRE SUMMIT, ADD AVALANCHE GEAR FOR TRUE SUMMIT

MAPS 82 J/14 SPRAY LAKES RESERVOIR, GEM TREK KANANASKIS LAKES

*As the name implies, this ridge is connected to Commonwealth Peak, and it is east and slightly north of its namesake. The ridge has three summits. The first is easily reached with snowshoes and allows for a wonderful summit panorama. The second is not so easily reached, requiring an ice axe and possibly crampons, but its summit view is phenomenal! The third and highest summit is only for those confident on steep snow and able to assess avalanche potential. The view is also phenomenal.*

## DIRECTIONS

The first part of the approach is the same as for Smuts Pass. Drive 2.2 km south of the Engadine Lodge turnoff and park on the west side of the road, around GR176312. Look west, across the flats of Smuts Creek, for a small gap in the trees (see the photo below). Snowshoe across the flats and go through the gap. The path trends slightly right before arriving at a "No camping/fires" sign. This is a very popular area so expect there to be a multitude of trails. As you approach the sign, go slightly left into the trees and head southwest. You'll soon arrive at another popular trail that runs north–south. The terrain opens up a little and the route should become more obvious.

At this point you should look for a cutline running southwest, south of Commonwealth Creek. To find it, follow the trail going toward the distinctive form of The Fist. The trail soon swings

COMMONWEALTH RIDGE FROM THE ROAD. C=CENTRE SUMMIT. N=NORTH SUMMIT. CP=COMMONWEALTH PEAK. PT=PIG'S TAIL. MB=MOUNT BIRDWOOD. SP=SMUTS PASS.

around to the left and then arrives at an open area, where it forks (GR168304). This fork is not always obvious. The right fork leads to Smuts Pass, the left to Commonwealth Lake – take the left.

Now you are at the northwest end of Commonwealth Ridge. Really, you can turn south anywhere around here and make your way up. However, it may be easier to follow the trail toward Commonwealth Lake. It winds its way uphill at a moderate grade, going southwest. Leave the trail when it turns slightly south (around GR166299), and head into the trees, making your way southeast and uphill. The grade is a little steeper here and switchbacking may make travel easier. Once you reach the very wide ridge, trend south. You've spent a fair amount of time in the trees and it's not over yet. Persevere up the north ridge to treeline. Finally the views start to open up. Throughout this approach and ascent look for other snowshoe trails heading in the right direction. Perhaps a group has made another trail up to the objective. Why break a new trail when you don't have to?

The north summit (more of a highpoint) is unmarked on most maps and lies at GR171289, 2368 m. To reach it you may have to circle around the ridge on the right (west) side and then make your way back up to the small highpoint. On a clear day, the views from this highpoint are fantastic. If the Kananaskis Range to the east doesn't leave your jaw hanging, nearby Commonwealth Peak, Mount Birdwood and Mount Smuts should do the trick.

### On to the centre summit

As good as the view from the north summit is, the one from the centre summit is far better, granting excellent views of the British Military Group. The ascent to the centre summit is also a far greater challenge than the one to the north summit. It is *not* a snowshoe ascent. An ice axe will be mandatory and crampons an asset. Your success will also depend on snow conditions and how much snow there is on the ridge. A route description is unnecessary. Simply

head up the narrowing ridge and follow it for about 500 m to the summit. Watch for cornices on your left and avalanche slopes on your right. A few steps are steep, but nothing too alarming and they are very short. The summit cairn (and its tremendous view) lies at GR172283, 2550 m. Return the way you came if the more challenging extension to the true summit is not on your agenda.

### Extension to the true summit of Commonwealth Ridge

The view from the true summit is slightly better than that from the centre summit. However, the path up to the summit can be significantly more dangerous than the one to the centre summit. This extension is for those experienced and comfortable on steep snow and good at assessing avalanche potential. With the right snow conditions the traverse can be completed without crampons, but I would not recommend it. Like the centre summit, however, the directions to the true summit are easy. Follow the ridge south to a daunting rock-band. Circumvent the rock-band on the right (west) side, staying close to the rock face. Again, be very mindful of avalanches here (**avalanche danger**). As soon as the ridge appears to the left, ascend steep slopes to reach it. The summit is only a few steps beyond (GR171281, 2561 m). The view of Commonwealth Peak's east face is amazing.

Do not attempt alternative descent routes from the true summit. There are many unseen cliffs, and you may get yourself into some very serious difficulties. Better to play it safe and return the same way. Back at the north summit, it is possible to take a more direct route back to your vehicle, descending east-facing slopes and then following Smuts Creek back to the flats. The avalanche rating should be low for this descent (**avalanche danger**). This direct route probably won't save you any time, though, as you may have to break new trail to get back to your vehicle. Note that there are some terrific Crazy Carpeting slopes on the east side of the peak. Again, be wary of avalanche danger.

THE IMPRESSIVE EAST FACE OF COMMONWEALTH PEAK.

# CHESTER LAKE AND SURROUNDING AREA

Chester Lake is without question the most popular snow-shoeing destination in Kananaskis. The lake is easily reached via a good snowshoe trail and is surrounded by spectacular mountains. For the more advanced snowshoer, there are several extensions to this trip, each granting outstanding views to the west. Due to the sheer volume of skiers, snowboarders and snowshoers making their way to Chester Lake, it is imperative that snowshoers use the official snowshoe trail and avoid the ski trail, except on a few short sections where the trail is shared.

MOUNT CHESTER AND CHESTER LAKE, AS SEEN FROM "LITTLE GALATEA."

# 28 CHESTER LAKE

(MAP 6, PAGE 316)

| | |
|---|---|
| DIFFICULTY EASY | |
| HAZARD LOW | |
| LAKE HEIGHT 2200 M | |
| ELEVATION GAIN 310 M | |
| ROUND TRIP DISTANCE 8 KM | |
| ROUND TRIP TIME 3–5 HOURS | |
| MAPS 82 J/14 SPRAY LAKES RESERVOIR, GEM TREK KANANASKIS LAKES | |

*The trip to Chester Lake is easy, scenic and has no objective hazards. Since the lake is also an extremely popular destination for skiers (both AT and cross country), a separate trail has been designated for snowshoers.*

## DIRECTIONS

Park at the Chester Lake parking lot. The first 400 m of the snowshoe trail is shared with the ski trail. It starts at the north end of the parking lot. Follow the trail for a short distance and take the left fork at the first intersection (well signed). After going over a bridge, look for the snowshoe trail sign on the right side of the trail. Turn right onto it and follow it through the forest and open areas to the beautiful environs of Chester Lake. There are trail signs on trees throughout to guide you. This trail gets very well packed down and some will opt to carry their snowshoes on their backpacks and hike to the Chester Lake area. However, snowshoes are excellent on descent, as they will prevent you from suddenly post-holing and possibly breaking a leg.

### Extension toward The Fortress

Continuing past Chester Lake and up into the valley toward The Fortress is generally safe if you don't venture too far up. Snowshoe past the lake (and the turnoff to the Three Lakes valley) on its north side and then go up through the trees into the upper valley. Once there, you can call it a day or continue toward the end of the valley. There are several house-sized boulders to see on the way. Avalanche danger from the sides increases as you travel farther up the valley. At the end of the valley a steep slope goes to The Fortress–Mount Chester col. This slope is very avalanche-prone and not recommended.

### Extension to Elephant Rocks and Three Lakes Valley

Like the previous sidetrip, this route is also relatively safe and very scenic. The turnoff for the valley is a few hundred metres along the northwest shore of the lake. Turn left and snowshoe toward the northwest. In another few hundred metres you'll arrive at a striking conglomeration of huge boulders known as Elephant Rocks. Past the rocks, continue going northwest for another 300–400 m and then swing around to the right (northeast) into the valley. Continue up the valley as far as you like, staying away from steep slopes that may have avalanche potential. This beautiful valley leads to the ascent slopes of Mount Galatea, which Alan Kane describes in *Scrambles in the Canadian Rockies*.

# 29 "LITTLE GALATEA"

(MAP 6, PAGE 316)

DIFFICULTY DIFFICULT

HAZARD HIGH

MOUNTAIN HEIGHT APPROX. 2675 M

ELEVATION GAIN APPROX. 800 M FROM PARKING LOT

ROUND-TRIP DISTANCE 12 KM

ROUND-TRIP TIME 6-9 HOURS

ADDITIONAL EQUIPMENT AVALANCHE GEAR,
ICE AXE AND POSSIBLY CRAMPONS

MAPS 82 J/14 SPRAY LAKES RESERVOIR,
GEM TREK KANANASKIS LAKES

*This minor highpoint sits at the southwest end of the Mount Galatea massif. The ascent is a much safer proposition than a winter ascent of "Little Chester" (see page 197) or Mount Chester, but you will still be exposed to potential avalanches from the sides. The view to the west is spectacular on a clear day.*

## DIRECTIONS

Follow the instructions to Chester Lake (see page 192). The ascent route is visible just before reaching Chester Lake. Look to the left (north) to view the route and asses its condition (see photo A opposite). Snowshoe directly toward the ascent gully. This will probably require wading through some pretty deep snow and will be very strenuous if you are alone. You will go through a short stint of trees and end up at a small lake. Snowshoe directly across the lake, or around it if you are not sure it's fully frozen, and then to the main ascent gully. This gully leads to a col between "Little Galatea" and the next highpoint of Mount Galatea. Don't be tempted to ascend slopes farther west: they are steeper and more avalanche-prone.

The first section of the gully is the steepest part (**avalanche danger**). If avalanches are a concern, stay to the right side of the gully and ascend through trees until you are above the steepest part. Invariably, this will be very strenuous, through deep and steep snow. Once level with or above the steep section in the gully, traverse into the gully and then continue up it. The grade is gentle in the gully, but the gully has steeper slopes on both sides. Those slopes will be your main concern for potential **avalanches**. Cornice failure to the left is also something to be cognizant of.

Nearing the col, the grade in the gully does become steeper,

[A] THE ASCENT ROUTE, AS SEEN FROM THE SMALL LAKE.
NOTE THE CORNICES LEFT OF THE LINE AND POTENTIAL
AVALANCHE SLOPES ON BOTH SIDES OF THE LINE. S=SUMMIT.

THE VIEW TO THE WEST. MOUNT SMUTS TO THE LEFT
AND MOUNT ASSINIBOINE, JUST RIGHT OF CENTRE.

THE VIEW TO THE WEST. MOUNT SMUTS TO THE LEFT AND MOUNT ASSINIBOINE, JUST RIGHT OF CENTRE.

and you should be wary if the slopes are wind-loaded and/or un-stable. Gain the col via the safest route and head easily to the summit to the west. Enjoy the outstanding view and return the same way. **Do not** descend the south ridge. Though scenic, this route will eventually force you onto steep terrain that could be very avalanche-prone and also challenging to descend.

# 30 "LITTLE CHESTER"

(MAP 6, PAGE 316)

**DIFFICULTY** DIFFICULT, SEVERE EXPOSURE TO AVALANCHE TERRAIN, MOUNTAINEERING

**HAZARD** HIGH

**MOUNTAIN HEIGHT** APPROX. 2650 M

**ELEVATION GAIN** APPROX. 775 M

**ROUND TRIP DISTANCE** 10 KM

**ROUND TRIP TIME** 5–9 HOURS

**ADDITIONAL EQUIPMENT** AVALANCHE GEAR, CRAMPONS, ICE AXE

**MAPS** 82 J/14 SPRAY LAKES RESERVOIR, GEM TREK KANANASKIS LAKES

*This trip out from Chester Lake is definitely the most dangerous one mentioned in this book. The route goes to the unnamed high-point west of Mount Chester, with the option to actually complete an ascent of Chester. This is prime avalanche terrain, and the ascent should only be undertaken with very stable conditions and by experienced parties. Many would consider this to be more mountaineering in nature than most of the trips described in this book. It is best to wait until May before making an attempt.*

### DIRECTIONS

Follow the directions to Chester Lake (see page 192). The route is obvious. From just before Chester Lake, snowshoe south and then southeast up to the col (**avalanche danger**). Be sure to assess and reassess the condition of this slope as you go up. It's very foreshortened and will probably take 1.5–2.5 hours to gain the col – that's a very long period of time to be exposed to avalanches!

At the col, turn right (west) and snowshoe to the highpoint and a wonderful view to the west. For an even better view, return to the col and then start up the northeast ridge of Mount Chester. If snow conditions are favourable, it is possible to ascend this ridge all the way to the summit. Again, this ascent is only for those with mountaineering experience. An ice axe will be mandatory for this ascent and crampons a strong recommendation. Also, this west-facing slope is often windblown early in the season and may have far less snow than the ascent to the col does. Return the same way.

THE AVALANCHE-PRONE ASCENT ROUTE TO LITTLE CHESTER,
AS SEEN FROM THE SOUTH END OF LITTLE GALATEA.
LC=LITTLE CHESTER. MC=MOUNT CHESTER.

# 31 HOGARTH LAKES

(MAP 6, PAGE 316)

| | |
|---|---|
| **DIFFICULTY** VERY EASY, MODERATE FOR THE EXTENSION | |
| **HAZARD** LOW, HIGH FOR THE EXTENSION | |
| **ELEVATION GAIN** NEGLIGIBLE, 180 M FOR THE EXTENSION | |
| **ROUND-TRIP DISTANCE** 4.5-KM LOOP, 5–7 KM FOR THE EXTENSION | |
| **ROUND-TRIP TIME** 2–4 HOURS, 3–5 HOURS FOR THE EXTENSION | |
| **ADDITIONAL EQUIPMENT** NONE FOR THE LAKES, AVALANCHE GEAR IF YOU GAIN ELEVATION ON THE OUTLIER | |
| **MAP** 82 J/14 SPRAY LAKE RESERVOIR, GEM TREK KANANASKIS LAKES | |

*The area around Hogarth and Mud lakes is probably the best area in the Canadian Rockies for beginner snowshoers. The loop route has a negligible amount of elevation gain, with no objective hazards, and there are infinite opportunities to go exploring should you feel like leaving the beaten path. For the adventurous, there is the option to gain some elevation (and a good view to the east) on the side of the east outlier of Commonwealth Peak.*

## DIRECTIONS

Park at Burstall Pass parking lot. Snowshoe the common trail west for 100 m or so, looking for the first orange snowshoe marker on the right side. Once you've found it, simply follow the markers as they take you west and then northwest toward the

Hogarth Lakes. For those who are new to snowshoeing and want to experience the joy (?) of trail-breaking, leave the well-trodden path at any time to do some exploring.

The markers take you to the northeast end of the Hogarth Lakes in about 2 km. At this point, the official trail turns south, following the east edge of both Hogarth Lakes. Follow the trail as it heads east and south back to the Burstall Pass trail, a few hundred metres from where you left the main trail initially.

## Extension Past Hogarth Lakes

*This extension of the Hogarth Lakes trip takes you in between an eastern outlier of Commonwealth Peak and a small, treed hill. For the best view, it is necessary to gain some elevation toward the ice climbs known as Parallel Falls. There is significant avalanche danger – take the necessary precautions.*

### Directions

From the northeast end of Hogarth Lakes, snowshoe west and then south, looking for the drainage between the outlier and the hill (GR11 618196E 5628379N, 1895 m). Ascend the fairly open drainage, going SSW and gaining some elevation. Stay in the drainage, even when a steep route to the right appears. This appears to be an old logging road, but it leads to a dead end.

Continue SSW to the base of an avalanche slope at GR11 617908E 5627972N, 1952 m. At the top of this slope are the ice climbs Parallel Falls. Views to the east start to improve, but gaining more elevation is required for the best view. If avalanche conditions are above "moderate," forgo the ascent to the ice climbs and continue following the valley up to the highest point and then down and southeast to Burstall Lakes. Old logging roads should make life easier. As you approach the first lake, look for the open path from the lake up to Burstall Pass Trail. Cross the first Burstall Lake, ascend to the trail and turn left (east). About 1.5 km of easy snowshoeing takes you back to the parking lot.

For those who want the best view of the day and have avalanche gear, ascend the right side of the avalanche slope (**avalanche danger**) mentioned at the beginning of the previous paragraph. Stay in or near the trees for a safer line. Go as high as you see fit, according to conditions. Going right up to the ice climbs is quite entertaining. After enjoying good views of Mount Galatea, Gusty Peak and Mount Chester, among others, return to the base of the avalanche slope. Return the way you came to get back to the parking lot, or complete the loop route as described above.

# 32 BURSTALL PASS

(MAP 6, PAGE 316)

| | |
|---|---|
| DIFFICULTY | MODERATE |
| HAZARD | MODERATE |
| PASS HEIGHT | 2380 M |
| ELEVATION GAIN | 470 M |
| ROUND-TRIP DISTANCE | 16 KM |
| ROUND-TRIP TIME | 5–8 HOURS |
| ADDITIONAL EQUIPMENT | AVALANCHE GEAR |
| MAPS | 82 J/14 SPRAY LAKE RESERVOIR, GEM TREK KANANASKIS LAKES |

*Like Chester Lake across the road, Burstall Pass is a very popular winter (and summer) destination. This 8-km trail is typically a skiers' trail. However, it is wide enough in most places for snowshoers to make their own trail. Be sure to do just that. Once out onto the flats the scenery is terrific, and for mountaineers there exists the options to ascend Snow Peak or, slightly easier, Burstall Pass Peak.*

## DIRECTIONS

Park at the Burstall Pass parking lot. There are several snowshoe trails in the area, though at present one doesn't exist for Burstall Pass. Therefore all users must share this trail. This is sometimes a problem after the first few major snowfalls of the season, when the bulk of trail-breaking duties must be shared. As soon as the trail becomes well established it is very wide and there's plenty of room for everyone. Be considerate of skiers and avoid stepping on their tracks. Sometimes there are ski tracks on either side, in which case the middle of the trail might be the best place for snowshoers. If no snowshoe tracks already exist, break trail on the right (north) side of the trail.

Follow the well-signed hiking trail. It heads west, turns to the left and uphill and then takes an immediate sharp right turn at another hiking sign. Ignore the orange snowshoeing signs along the way. Several kilometres along (when you are level with the east side of Commonwealth Peak) there are two paths you can take.

The first option is to descend to the right, down to Burstall Flats. At the flats, turn west and snowshoe to the end and another trail sign. Stay on the left (south) side of the flats. This is the recommended route for snowshoers.

If you don't descend to the flats, continue along Burstall Pass Trail. The trail narrows and then winds its way through trees and down to the flats. Getting across the flats to the headwall is an easy affair. Simply follow the trail signs. Don't veer off to the right to the drainage beneath Mount Birdwood and Pig's Tail. This drainage is used by skiers on descent.

The last trail sign is right in front of the trees of the headwall. The trail enters the forest, weaves its way up the headwall and eventually emerges in open terrain south of Mount Birdwood and east of Snow Peak. Follow the valley as it curves around to the south. You'll soon enter the trees again, but only for a short time. The terrain ascends through a short canyon-like area and then out into more open slopes east of Burstall Pass. Try to stay to the east to avoid steeper, avalanche-prone slopes east of Burstall Pass and Snow Peak. The farther south you go, the less steep the terrain to the pass becomes. Eventually you can turn west and snowshoe easily to the pass and a wonderful viewpoint.

If Snow Peak or Burstall Pass Peak isn't on your agenda, return the same way. When you arrive at the top of the headwall, **do not** use the skier's descent drainage.

# 33 SNOW PEAK

(MAP 6, PAGE 316)

| | |
|---|---|
| DIFFICULTY | DIFFICULT VIA BURSTALL PASS AND THE SOUTH RIDGE |
| HAZARD | HIGH |
| MOUNTAIN HEIGHT | 2789 M |
| ELEVATION GAIN | 900 M FROM THE PARKING LOT |
| ROUND-TRIP DISTANCE | 20 KM |
| ROUND-TRIP TIME | 9–12 HOURS |
| ADDITIONAL EQUIPMENT | AVALANCHE GEAR, CRAMPONS, ICE AXE |
| MAPS | 82 J/14 SPRAY LAKE RESERVOIR, GEM TREK KANANASKIS LAKES |

*The winter view from the summit of Snow Peak is sensational. The ascent starts at Burstall Pass and puts you on steep avalanche slopes, so wait for good snow stability before attempting this trip. Take an ice axe, crampons and your camera! Note that this peak is not identified on most maps.*

## DIRECTIONS

Follow the instructions to Burstall Pass (see page 202). Good views of Snow Peak are frequently seen throughout this approach and you should have plenty of time to start thinking about the safety of the route. At the pass, turn to the north and follow the south ridge of Snow Peak to the summit (**avalanche danger**). You may need an ice axe and crampons to ascend steeper slopes higher up and small rock-bands. The alternative is to traverse to the left around these obstacles. This means going onto terrain that could

BURSTALL PASS IS A VERY POPULAR BACKCOUNTRY SKIING DESTINATION. NOTICE THE ABUNDANCE OF SKIERS' DOWN-TRACKS. SP=SUMMIT OF SNOW PEAK. MB=MOUNT BIRDWOOD.

definitely avalanche. Use discretion and back down if the stability is not "bomber." Always try to return to the ridge, but be very wary of huge cornices hanging off the east side of the peak. The grade eases higher up and the summit is quickly reached. When you have finished salivating at the views toward Sir Douglas, Birdwood and Assiniboine, return the same way.

# 34 "BURSTALL PASS PEAK"

(MAP 6, PAGE 316)

| | |
|---|---|
| DIFFICULTY MODERATE | |
| HAZARD MODERATE | |
| MOUNTAIN HEIGHT 2615 M | |
| ELEVATION GAIN 700 M FROM THE PARKING LOT | |
| ROUND-TRIP DISTANCE 18 KM | |
| ROUND-TRIP TIME 8–10 HOURS | |
| ADDITIONAL EQUIPMENT AVALANCHE GEAR, POSSIBLY CRAMPONS AND ICE AXE | |
| MAPS 82 J/14 SPRAY LAKE RESERVOIR, 82 J/11 KANANASKIS LAKES, GEM TREK KANANASKIS LAKES | |

*This peak is an excellent extension of the Burstall Pass trip and is a little safer than Snow Peak. However, you will still be required to ascend a few short avalanche slopes and a couple of steeper sections. If you do the north–south traverse, you'll feel good if you have crampons and an ice axe for one narrow section of the summit ridge.*

## DIRECTIONS

If this peak is the only intended goal for the day, it is not necessary to go all the way to Burstall Pass, although the added distance is negligible. From Burstall Pass (see page 202), go southwest to gain the north ridge of Burstall Pass Peak. Follow the ridge south. A short but steep rock-band can be tackled head-on (if the snow is stable) or circumvented by going around the right side (recommended). Once past this obstacle, follow the ridge to join up with one of the two routes to the summit described below.

If you choose not to take the Burstall Pass route, you can make a more direct route toward the summit once out onto the open slopes east of Burstall Pass (see photo A below). This direct route is a little steeper than the route from the pass and will expose you to an additional, if short-lived, avalanche slope. Gain the lower ridge (terrace) via this steep slope, which sits to the left of an obvious rock-band. At this point, you have a choice of routes: a north–south traverse or an easy route.

### North–South Traverse (avalanche danger)

If the snow stability is good and you don't mind traversing a narrow ridge, the best route from this point is to follow the scenic north ridge to the false summit. One section of this ridge is steep and will require caution. At the false summit (big cairn) continue south along the ridge. Soon the ridge narrows, although it appears

[A] THE WONDERFUL ENVIRONS AROUND BURSTALL PASS, AND VARIOUS ROUTES UP BURSTALL PASS PEAK. ER=EASY ROUTE. DR=DIFFICULT ROUTE. RB=ROCK-BAND. FS=FALSE SUMMIT. C=CRUX. TS=TRUE SUMMIT.

far worse than it really is. Most will want to take off their snow-shoes for this section and use an ice axe and crampons if necessary. The summit and its incredible view are a short distance beyond this section. To descend, continue south along the ridge for a short distance until you can escape down easy slopes to the east. Do not descend all the way to the bottom of the valley. Instead, stay high on the upper terrace and go north, back to your ascent route.

### Easy route

If conditions are suspect, or you simply want the easiest and safest route to the summit, traverse south on the lower ridge. The ridge parallels the summit ridge, going past the actual summit. When it becomes obvious, make a sharp right (northwest) and head easily to the summit. On a clear day, the summit view will not disappoint. Return the same way.

# 35 MOUNT JELLICOE

(MAP 6, MAP 7, PAGES 316 AND 317)

DIFFICULTY DIFFICULT, MOUNTAINEERING
HAZARD HIGH
MOUNTAIN HEIGHT 3075 M
ELEVATION GAIN 1450 M
ROUND-TRIP DISTANCE APPROX. 28 KM
ROUND-TRIP TIME 12–14 HOURS
ADDITIONAL EQUIPMENT AVALANCHE GEAR,
CRAMPONS, ICE AXE, POSSIBLY A ROPE AND
SLINGS FOR THE SUMMIT RIDGE
MAPS 82 J/14 SPRAY LAKE RESERVOIR, 82 J/11
KANANASKIS LAKES, GEM TREK KANANASKIS LAKES

*Mount Jellicoe is a little bit lower than its neighbours, French, Robertson and Sir Douglas, but it still offers a sensational view. The ascent is relatively straightforward, although very lengthy and extremely strenuous physically. Avalanches can be a serious concern on this mountain, and you may want a rope to traverse the narrow summit ridge. This trip is for very experienced and fit parties who are comfortable on glaciers, long sections of steep snow and an exposed summit ridge.*

## DIRECTIONS

Park at the Burstall Pass parking lot on Highway 742. Snowshoe or hike the first few hundred metres of Burstall Pass Trail. The trail quickly turns to the left, going uphill, and forks at the top. The wide right branch is the continuation of Burstall Pass. Take the left fork, which goes gently uphill for a distance and then descends to French Creek. Yet again, this is a popular trail for skiers. Do your best to avoid direct contact with their tracks. Though the summer trail is easy to follow, the winter one can change location. Sometimes there are tracks crossing French Creek immediately and then running parallel to the creek on its left (east) side, and sometimes the trail stays on the west side of the creek, crossing to the east several hundred metres upcreek. Either way they end up in the same place – on the east side.

Follow French Creek south, sometimes right alongside the creek, sometimes farther away. Again, it changes from year to year. If you are really unlucky, you'll have to break trail all the way up! The beautiful forms of mounts Sir Douglas and Robertson soon appear in front of you. Much farther up the creek the route goes up and to the left and then continues to parallel the creek, but high above it. The general route is fairly obvious even if you are not following any tracks or a trail.

The valley eventually turns more to the south. Here lies the French Glacier. This glacier is considered to be relatively safe by most people. However, it does have crevasses. Rope up to avoid an embarrassing (or deadly) fall into one. Slog your way up the glacier between the striking forms of Robertson and French and gain the Haig Glacier. You should be 3–4 hours into the trip at this point, and the Haig Glacier is a good place to take a break and enjoy the surrounding area.

Shapely Mount Jellicoe is entirely visible at the left (east) side of the glacier from this vantage point (see photo). Descend the Haig Glacier for about 2 km, staying relatively near to Jellicoe. You'll lose 140 vertical m along the way. The goal at this point is to ascend the southwest slopes of Jellicoe or traverse east directly to the south ridge. If avalanches are a concern, gaining the south ridge as soon as possible is recommended. Before you start the ascent, trade your snowshoes for crampons and an ice axe.

NEAR THE TOP OF THE HAIG GLACIER, WITH THE PICTURESQUE
FORM OF MOUNT JELLICOE BEHIND. MJ=MOUNT JELLICOE.
AF=SLOPES OF THE SOUTHWEST SIDE OF JELLICOE
TO AIM FOR WHEN BEGINNING THE ASCENT.

The southwest slopes are prime avalanche terrain (**avalanche danger**). Gain some elevation up these slopes, and, when it becomes feasible, head east to intercept the south ridge. Follow the south ridge up to the false summit. Watch for cornices. The traverse from the false summit to the true one is not long but is very exposed for a few sections. Some of the traverse can be made on the left side of the ridge but eventually you must return to the ridge proper. Determining whether you are standing on the snow-covered ridge or part of the cornice can be tricky. Rope up and belay if necessary. There are a few good rock horns to sling for belays.

If you reach the summit in cloudy conditions, or even worse a whiteout, all that energy will be for naught! The panorama on a clear day is tremendous. Mountains of the French Group, Opal Range, British Military Group, Royal Group, Elk Range and Spray Mountains surround you. Take in the splendour and then return the same way. The return trip will be long and very taxing physically. Prepare yourself!

### Option: the north ridge of Mount Maude

If unfavourable conditions and lack of time and/or energy conspire to preclude your ascent of Mount Jellicoe, a short section of Mount Maude's north ridge makes a good alternative. The ascent is straightforward and the highpoint provides a good view. From the point where the French Glacier meets the Haig Glacier in the directions above, simply cross the Haig Glacier, going south and slightly west, toward the obvious hump (see photo). Follow the initially wide ridge south for as long as conditions and your comfort level warrant. Terminate your ascent at any one of several highpoints on the ridge. Eventually the terrain becomes technical and you will have to turn around. Return the same way you came.

ABOVE OPPOSITE: MOUNT JELLICOE'S EXPOSED SUMMIT RIDGE. BELOW OPPOSITE: AT THE TOP OF THE HAIG GLACIER, WITH MOUNT MAUDE'S LONG AND INTRICATE NORTH RIDGE STRETCHED OUT BEHIND. NR=NORTH RIDGE. MM=MOUNT MAUDE. (PHOTO BY FERENC JASCO)

# 36 WARSPITE LAKE

(MAP 7, PAGE 317)

| | |
|---|---|
| DIFFICULTY EASY | |
| HAZARD LOW | |
| LAKE HEIGHT 1820 M | |
| ELEVATION GAIN 120 M | |
| ROUND TRIP DISTANCE 4 KM | |
| ROUND TRIP TIME 2–4 HOURS | |
| MAPS 82 J/11 KANANASKIS LAKES, GEM TREK KANANASKIS LAKES | |

*This is an easy and popular trip that is perfect for beginners. Getting some exercise may be the primary motivation for this trip, as the scenery is not particularly spellbinding. However, for more experienced snowshoers with avalanche gear, the option to continue up to the scenic environs of Warspite Cirque provides a healthy serving of beautiful scenery. For those who really want a workout and a terrific view, there is also the option to snowshoe and then scramble up to Warspite Ridge.*

## DIRECTIONS

Park at the Black Prince parking lot near the south end of Highway 742. The interpretive trail is well marked and easy to follow. In summer the trail winds through light forest and within minutes crosses Smith-Dorrien Creek. In winter there is often a small shortcut to the left that crosses the creek over a snow bridge. Both trails quickly unite and then a long uphill grind starts, heading to the right. The slope is not terribly steep and travel will be easy.

At the top of the hill sits a bench (probably half-submerged in snow). Stay right and keep following the trail as you lose a chunk of the elevation you just gained. Again stay right when you arrive at a hiking trail sign. There could be a multitude of other ski and snow-shoe trails – it's best to just follow the most prominent one. It's only about 10 minutes from the hiking trail sign to Warspite Lake.

The actual lake is more like a big puddle and will probably fail to impress. Of more interest is the massive form of Mount Black Prince, looming above the lake. To the left of the lake, much of the route to Warspite Cirque is visible. Even if you have no desire to visit the cirque, it is worth your while to wander over to the southwest side of the lake and through a small group of trees. Beyond the trees the scenery opens up again to some beautiful vistas. Return the same way or go to the next trip for the continuation to Warspite Cirque.

A SUMMER-TIME LOOK AT WARSPITE LAKE (PUDDLE).
I DOUBT LAKE ONTARIO IS FEELING THREATENED!
MOUNT BLACK PRINCE BEHIND THE LAKE.

# 37 WARSPITE CIRQUE

(MAP 7, PAGE 317)

| | |
|---|---|
| DIFFICULTY | MODERATE |
| HAZARD | HIGH |
| CIRQUE HEIGHT | 2170 M |
| ELEVATION GAIN | 450 M |
| ROUND-TRIP DISTANCE | 8 KM |
| ROUND-TRIP TIME | 4–6 HOURS |
| ADDITIONAL EQUIPMENT | AVALANCHE GEAR |
| MAPS | 82 J/11 KANANASKIS LAKES, GEM TREK KANANASKIS LAKES |

*The scenery en route to and around Warspite Cirque is far superior to that of Warspite Lake. There are some avalanche slopes that must be ascended, so wait for good stability and take avalanche gear and some friends to dig you out if necessary!*

## DIRECTIONS

Follow the directions to Warspite Lake (see page 214). Cross the lake or snowshoe around the left side toward the far end. Just before getting there, cut to the left through a short stint of trees to arrive at more open terrain. Most of the route to the cirque is now visible (see photo A opposite).

Snowshoe southwest, passing through another group of trees, over a big flat rock pile, through yet another very small stand of trees and then out into the open again. This is not the only route to the ascent slope, but it is probably the most direct one.

The crux of the trip is now before you (see photo B on page 218). Curve around to the right and then left as you search for

[A] THE APPROXIMATE ROUTE TO WARSPITE CIRQUE,
AS SEEN FROM JUST BEYOND WARSPITE LAKE.

the safest route up. Weaving through the small trees may be best. The right side can be threatened by avalanche hazard from above, so don't go too far west. You are basically following the direction of Warspite Creek but also staying west of the creek. Soon the terrain becomes considerably steeper and avalanches are a greater concern (**avalanche danger**). If stability is good, it's a relatively short but steep ascent to the upper cirque (photo B). Staying in the trees is a good idea but trail-breaking can be brutally strenuous. Trend to the left as you ascend.

The first sight upon entering the cirque is the aesthetic form of Mount Warspite at the far south end. As you venture farther south into the hanging valley, two possible extensions of the trip become obvious. If either of these appeals to you and your group, go to the next trip, Warspite Ridge. If not, enjoy the beautiful surroundings and then return the same way.

ABOVE: [B] POTENTIAL ROUTES TO THE CIRQUE. WC=WARSPITE CASCADES. BELOW: ENTERING WARSPITE CIRQUE, WITH THE FORMIDABLE FORM OF MOUNT WARSPITE AHEAD.

# 38 WARSPITE RIDGE

(MAP 7, PAGE 317)

| | |
|---|---|
| DIFFICULTY | DIFFICULT |
| HAZARD | HIGH |
| RIDGE HEIGHT | 2582 M |
| ELEVATION GAIN | 850 M |
| ROUND-TRIP DISTANCE | 11 KM |
| ROUND-TRIP TIME | 6–8 HOURS |
| ADDITIONAL EQUIPMENT | AVALANCHE GEAR, POSSIBLY CRAMPONS AND ICE AXE FOR SUMMIT BLOCK |
| MAPS | 82 J/11 KANANASKIS LAKES, GEM TREK KANANASKIS LAKES |

*Reaching the summit of Warspite Ridge will provide some very sweet icing on the cake of what is already a terrific trip to Warspite Lake and Warspite Cirque (see pages 214 and 216). The ascent goes up a 25–30° snow slope and then requires some rock scrambling to the top. As usual, avalanche gear and stable snow conditions are a must. A much safer, but less rewarding, option is to ascend the ridge on the west side of the valley instead.*

## DIRECTIONS

Follow the directions to Warspite Lake (page 214) and then to Warspite Cirque (page 216). Upon arriving at Warspite Cirque, travel south toward Mount Warspite, looking left for the correct ascent slope. The summit is not visible from the cirque and lies slightly to the right (south) of the highest-looking point. There are several potential routes to the ridge, but the easiest and least steep slope starts around GR257166, 2304 m (see photo A on next page).

[A] THE TWO ROUTES UP TO THE SUMMIT OF WARSPITE RIDGE.
ER=EASIEST ROUTE. AR=ALTERNATIVE ROUTE.

Be sure to pick the right one. Adjacent slopes to the north are much steeper and will probably require crampons and an ice axe.

Ascend 250 vertical m to the col at GR262167, 2560 m (**avalanche danger**). The summit is a short distance away to the north (GR262168, 2582 m). Depending on snow conditions, the summit may or may not be accessible. Regardless, some slightly exposed rock scrambling is required to reach it. Crampons and an axe may be of assistance if the summit block is covered in snow and ice. Room at the top is very limited, and as always, be aware of a cornice on the east side. On a clear day the view is excellent, especially the impressive form of Mount Warspite looming above the ridge. Return the same way.

## ALTERNATIVE OBJECTIVE: RIDGE TO THE WEST OF WARSPITE CIRQUE

*As stated earlier, the low ridge on the west side of Warspite Cirque makes a decent alternative objective when conditions are not good for Warspite Ridge.*

## DIRECTIONS

Upon entering the cirque, continue going south until you see an obvious route up, to your right. Snowshoe up reasonably angled terrain until you reach the ridge. The ridge overlooks Black Prince Tarns. Follow the ridge north until you reach a highpoint or until you've had enough, and then retrace your steps back to the cirque. Unless you encounter one that is brutally obvious, do not try any shortcuts back to the cirque.

Even though it may look tempting, **do not** under any circumstances try to ascend slopes to the col on the west side of Mount Warspite. This is the difficult scramble route outlined an Alan Kane's *Scrambles in the Canadian Rockies* and is extremely dangerous in winter.

# KENT RIDGE AND LAWSON RIDGE

The Kananaskis Range is home to numerous spectacular peaks, including the popular scrambles Mount Chester, The Fortress and Mount Galatea. The south end of the range terminates in two long ridges that resemble tines of a fork. Although Mount Lawson, on the east side, and Mount Kent, on the west, are the only official peaks present, there are at least five worthwhile routes to various highpoints along the ridges. Each route sports a wonderful summit panorama. The best view, and not surprisingly the most strenuous and difficult trip of the group, can be taken in from the summit of Kent Ridge North. Wait for a clear day and stable snow conditions to do this ascent.

AT THE COL BETWEEN KENT RIDGE NORTH
OUTLIER AND KENT RIDGE NORTH.

# 39 SAWMILL LOOP

(MAP 6, MAP 7, PAGES 316 AND 317)

| | |
|---|---|
| DIFFICULTY EASY | |
| HAZARD LOW | |
| ELEVATION GAIN 120 M | |
| ROUND-TRIP DISTANCE 5.1 KM | |
| ROUND-TRIP TIME 2–3 HOURS | |
| MAPS 82 J/14 SPRAY LAKE RESERVOIR, 82 J/11 KANANASKIS LAKES, GEM TREK KANANASKIS LAKES | |

*The Sawmill Loop is another good beginner trip. The trail is generally easy to follow (although as of 2010 it had become overgrown in places) and avalanche hazard is non-existent. However, the views are quite limited. Consider extending your trip to include the first part of Kent Ridge North Outlier (up to treeline) if the weather is good and you looking for a fine view. The loop can be completed in either direction, but counter-clockwise is recommended and described below.*

## DIRECTIONS

Park at the Sawmill parking lot, near the south end of Highway 742. Depending on the time of the year, this parking lot may be closed. If that is the case, park at the Sawmill turnoff. Snowshoe to the actual parking area. The Kent Ridge North Outlier is clearly visible from the parking area, and you may want to make note of it, in case you decide to head in that direction instead (see next trip). Note that getting to the summit of the outlier may require avalanche gear.

Find the trailhead at the north end of the parking lot and start up. Pass a gate and look for the first orange snowshoe marker straight ahead. The other paths are ski trails. Follow the path to the second orange marker, where the trail swings around to the left. After gaining some elevation, the trail forks again at the third marker. Follow this one as the trail swings around to the left (go right for Kent Ridge North Outlier). You have gained most of the elevation at this point, and for the next 2 km the trail heads northwest, at pretty much the same elevation.

Near the top of the loop, the trail crosses James Walker Creek. Shortly after, at approximately GR232253, the trail turns almost completely around and starts back toward the parking lot, but on the west side of James Walker Creek. Expect to cross the creek several more times on the return leg of the trip.

THE EAST SIDE OF GR244254, HAVING ALMOST DESCENDED TO THE OUTLIER/KENT RIDGE NORTH COL.

# 40 KENT RIDGE NORTH OUTLIER

(MAP 6, MAP 7, PAGES 316 AND 317)

| | |
|---|---|
| DIFFICULTY | MODERATE |
| HAZARD | MODERATE, LOW IF THE SUMMIT RIDGE IS BLOWN FREE OF SNOW |
| SUMMIT HEIGHT | 2550 M |
| ELEVATION GAIN | 725 M |
| ROUND-TRIP DISTANCE | 6.5 KM |
| ROUND-TRIP TIME | 4–6 HOURS |
| ADDITIONAL EQUIPMENT | AVALANCHE GEAR |
| MAPS | 82 J/14 SPRAY LAKE RESERVOIR, 82 J/11 KANANASKIS LAKES, GEM TREK KANANASKIS LAKES |

*This is one of my favourite snowshoe trips. For a small peak, the views are terrific and the potential for amazing cornice scenery is great. Routefinding through a maze of cutlines and old roads to the south ridge is definitely the crux of the trip. Wait for a clear day.*

## DIRECTIONS

Park at the Sawmill parking lot, near the south end of Highway 742. Depending on the time of the year, this parking lot may be closed. If that is the case, park at the Sawmill turnoff. Snowshoe to the actual parking area. The objective sits NNW of the parking lot and is clearly visible. Take a good look to see approximately how much snow is up there (see photo on next page). The west-facing slope is subject to being windblown.

Find the trailhead at the north end of the parking lot and start up. Pass a gate and look for the first orange snowshoe marker straight ahead. The other paths are ski trails. Follow the path to the second orange marker, where the trail swings around to the left. After gaining some elevation, the trail forks again at the third marker. This time take the right fork (GR11 624114E 5623630N, 1907 m). The left fork is the continuation of the official snowshoe route.

Now that you've left the official trail, routefinding to the south ridge becomes a little trickier. There is a maze of old cutlines switchbacking the southwest side of the peak. Taking the wrong one is easy and although a mistake won't necessarily mean the end of your day, getting back on track may require some very strenuous trail-breaking through the bush. I provide specific GR references here for those who like using GPS.

When the cutline forks again, after you leave the official snowshoe trail, take the left fork (11 624212E 5623633N, 1923 m).

KENT RIDGE NORTH OUTLIER, AS SEEN
FROM THE SAWMILL PARKING LOT.

Continue up switchbacks to GR11 624221E 5623903N, 1986 m. At this point, the trail takes a hard right and follows a long switchback, going southeast, all the way to the south ridge. It then starts to curve left. Look for flagging in trees to offer specific directions, but in general you'll want to trend left (north) up the treed south ridge.

If you and your group are the first in the area, expect to do some strenuous trail-breaking. The following GR numbers will help:

11 624405E 5623856N, 2048 m

11 624412E 5623901N, 2051 m

11 624374E 5624023N, 2103 m

11 624361E 5624227N, 2180 m

The final GR number in this list should put you at treeline on the south ridge. The remainder of the route is a simple ridgewalk to the summit.

Snowshoes may or may not be necessary, but I recommended you carry them with you in case you decide to take the alternative descent route. The ridge is subject to high winds and may be windblown – hence some great cornice scenery to the right. If the ridge is plastered in deep snow, keep your snowshoes on. Starting an avalanche while ascending the ridge is not likely but it is not completely outside the realm of possibility either. Take precautions just in case.

Once you see the summit view, the temptation to continue to Kent Ridge North (a far superior viewpoint) will probably be strong. If that's the plan, continue on to the next trip, keeping in mind that stable snow conditions will be essential. If the outlier was enough, return the same way. Alternative descent routes present significant avalanche danger and are therefore not recommended.

TYPICAL SCENERY ON THE RIDGE. KENT RIDGE NORTH TO THE RIGHT.

# 41 KENT RIDGE NORTH

(MAP 6, MAP 7, PAGES 316 AND 317)

| | |
|---|---|
| DIFFICULTY DIFFICULT | |
| HAZARD HIGH | |
| SUMMIT HEIGHT 2914 M | |
| ELEVATION GAIN 1200 M | |
| ROUND-TRIP DISTANCE 9 KM | |
| ROUND-TRIP TIME 9–12 HOURS | |
| ADDITIONAL EQUIPMENT AVALANCHE GEAR, CRAMPONS, ICE AXE | |
| MAPS 82 J/14 SPRAY LAKE RESERVOIR, 82 J/11 KANANASKIS LAKES, GEM TREK KANANASKIS LAKES | |

*This unofficial summit is definitely the highlight of the Kent and Lawson ridges. The ascent is long, strenuous, at times tedious, and includes sections of high objective hazards. Stable snow conditions and perfectly clear skies are a must for this trip. The described route first visits the Kent Ridge North Outlier (see page 225). If things aren't looking good for the true summit of Kent Ridge North, the outlier is an excellent consolation prize.*

## DIRECTIONS

Follow the route description to the Kent Ridge North Outlier, at GR244254 (see page 225). Kent Ridge North is the obvious peak to the east. The crux of the trip is getting down to the col between an outlier and Kent Ridge North. Depending on snow conditions, this descent may be a relatively easy affair or it could involve descending and traversing steep avalanche slopes.

Start down toward the col and arrive immediately at a steep rock-band. Here you must lose elevation on either side of the ridge and look for a safe place to traverse back to the ridge. If the snow is bomber, the right (south) side of the ridge works best. Descend steep avalanche-prone slopes (**avalanche danger**), until it is easy to traverse north, back to the ridge. If you are very confident on steep snow with snowshoes, keep them on. Otherwise trade the shoes for crampons and an ice axe.

If the snow on the south side of the ridge is in any way suspect, lose elevation down to the left (north) side and look for a safe place to descend the rock-band. This terrain is definitely not for snowshoes and will require going on foot, preferably with crampons. Again, an ice axe is mandatory here. Once through the band, traverse back to the ridge (**avalanche danger**).

At the col, contemplate the remaining 450 vertical m to the summit and then start up. The route is obvious but the slope is very foreshortened. Expect to take 1.5–2 hours to ascend this. Be aware of snow conditions, as the gradient is steep enough to avalanche. As well as offering a magnificent panorama, the summit will be lined with huge cornices. Stay well clear of the edge.

An alternative and easier descent route does exist but it will require very stable snow conditions. If such is not the case, return the same way you came. For the alternative route, descend to the col and then turn to the northwest and descend the obvious slope (drainage) toward James Walker Creek. Follow the safest line, but trend over to the left side of the creek when it appears. Staying in the trees when possible will also reduce your chances of getting caught in a slide. Near the bottom, intercept the James Walker Creek trail, turn left onto it and follow it south, back to the Sawmill parking lot.

ABOVE: Traversing very steep slopes on the north side
of GR244254. BELOW: Mark atop the summit cairn.

KEVIN BARTON AND MARK NUGARA POWER UP THE LOWER SLOPES
OF KENT RIDGE NORTH.

# 42 KENT RIDGE SOUTH

(MAP 7, PAGE 317)

| | |
|---|---|
| DIFFICULTY | MODERATE |
| HAZARD | MODERATE |
| SUMMIT HEIGHT | 2400–2635 M |
| ELEVATION GAIN | 600 M FOR THE LOWER SUMMIT; 835 M FOR THE HIGHER SUMMIT |
| ROUND-TRIP DISTANCE | 3–5 KM |
| ROUND-TRIP TIME | 8–10 HOURS |
| ADDITIONAL EQUIPMENT | AVALANCHE GEAR |
| MAPS | 82 J/11 KANANASKIS LAKES, GEM TREK KANANASKIS LAKES |

*There are at least three routes to the south end of Kent Ridge. Each one is very similar in character and differs only in steepness and length – the longer the route the flatter. Routes 1 and 2 are recommended if your only objective is the south peak of the south ridge. If you intend to go north along Kent Ridge toward the summit of Mount Kent, Route 3 is the shortest route, although all three will work.*

## DIRECTIONS

### Route 1 (least steep)

Drive about 1 km west of the Peninsula day-use area parking lot on Highway 742. Park on the north side of the road, just past an unnamed creek that comes down from Kent Ridge. The first part of the ascent is the most strenuous because you must climb over deadfall and weave your way up the forested ridge, going northwest. Either stick to the ridge or use the creek as an ascent route, whichever is the easiest. Higher up, the ridge and terrain trend a little to the left. You are aiming for the first highpoint at GR288192, 2360 m. Even at a relatively low elevation, this highpoint, sandwiched between the British Military Group to the west and the Opal Range to the east, offers a splendid view in all directions. If you wish to continue the trip, go to "Extension to the South Ridge of Mount Kent" (see page 235). Otherwise return the same way.

### Route 2 (slightly steeper than route 1)

Drive about 2.5 km west of the Peninsula day-use area parking lot on Highway 742. Park on the north side of the road, just past the unmarked Blackshade Creek, which comes down from Kent Ridge. Follow the direction of the creek on its left (west) side, heading due north. As is the case with Route 1, the first section through the trees is the most strenuous part of the trip. Stay well west of the creek and make your way to the first highpoint at GR288192, 2360 m. Although only about 1.5 km in horizontal distance and about 600 m of vertical gain, this ascent will probably take longer than you might expect. Enjoy a pretty decent summit view before making your next decision. If you wish to continue the trip, go to the trip extension: South Ridge of Mount Kent" (see facing page). Otherwise, return the same way.

### Route 3 (similar to route 2, bypasses first highpoint if desired)

Park at the Black Prince parking lot or on the east side of the road, opposite the parking entrance. The objective is to make your way up the large, treed, west-facing slope between drainages. From the road, head northeast, uphill. Don't go too far to the right; you may end up on avalanche terrain near the south drainage. Follow the natural contour of the slope, aiming for the south end of the ridge at GR285202, 2400 m. Once there, the highpoint at GR288192, 2360 m can be reached easily by going southeast. Otherwise, turn left (north) and follow the south ridge of Mount

Kent. Be wary of cornices on the east side of the ridge. The ridge may be windblasted, making snowshoes unnecessary.

### Extension to the south ridge of Mount Kent

Having reached the highpoint at GR288192, start going north-west and descend a little to a col. Then, go up to the south ridge of Mount Kent. Watching for cornices along the way, keep ascending the south ridge for as long as you see fit. If travel is easy, it is possible to go almost to the summit of Mount Kent. Depending on conditions, this traverse may require crampons and an ice axe instead of snowshoes. Just before the true summit of Mount Kent you will reach another highpoint. This will probably be the end of the line for most. The summit of Kent is several hundred metres to the north, but ascending to it includes traversing some difficult and dangerous terrain, including one steep rock-band. Whether you make it to the true summit or not, return the same way you came. Although it is possible to descend west-facing slopes directly to the road, this terrain is very steep and avalanche-prone and is therefore not recommended.

# 43 GYPSUM RIDGE

(MAP 7, PAGE 317)

| | |
|---|---|
| DIFFICULTY | MODERATE |
| HAZARD | LOW |
| RIDGE HEIGHT | 2100 M |
| ELEVATION GAIN | 500 M |
| ROUND-TRIP DISTANCE | 6 KM |
| ROUND-TRIP TIME | 2.5–5 HOURS |
| MAPS | 82 J/11 KANANASKIS LAKES, GEM TREK KANANASKIS LAKES |

*In some ways Gypsum Ridge is a "classic" snowshoe trip, as the heavily treed terrain is not conducive to skiing. Snowshoes are by far the best mode of winter transportation here. The selling point of this trip is the great view of Lower Kananaskis Lake and its surrounding peaks. However, to experience this view you have to wait until you are almost at the summit. Practically the entire ascent stays amidst view-blocking trees.*

## DIRECTIONS

From Kananaskis Lakes Trail, turn onto Highway 742 (Smith-Dorrien). As you pass the Peninsula turnoff, Gypsum Ridge is the treed hill in front of you. Continue northwest for 3.1 km and then pull off to the west side of the road, where the barricade ends (GR290177). Much of the route is visible from the road. It is highly unlikely you will be inspired by this view – trees, trees and more trees! (See photo A opposite.)

From the road, snowshoe due south toward Smith-Dorrien Creek, losing 80 m of elevation as you go. It's about 500 horizontal m to the creek. Cross the creek and continue heading south, this time uphill. The bulk of the work is now in front of you. This is a fairly popular route. As such it may be worth your while to search around a little for a previously broken trail right after you cross the creek. You'll probably feel like you have just won the lottery if you find one!

If not, the trail-breaking up to the west ridge of the objective could be very strenuous – prepare yourself and the large group you have recruited to help share trail-breaking duties! The ascent slope alternates sections of gentle terrain with much steeper ones, though there is nothing unreasonable throughout. Keep working your way up and south until you intersect the wide Gypsum Mine road. You can follow this road for a short while, but you'll soon have to leave it to head southeast to gain the west ridge. It is best to do this early and stay on the north side of the wide, treed ridge. GPS waypoints are provided below for those who wish to use them.

[A] THE SOMEWHAT BORING-LOOKING ASCENT ROUTE UP GYPSUM RIDGE. R=ROAD. S=SUMMIT.

Once you are convinced you are on the west ridge – it may not be obvious because of the heavy tree cover and undulating terrain – turn left (east) and make your way along the ridge. It eventually becomes much narrower, though it is not at all exposed. Again, you may find travel on the north side of the ridge a little easier.

You'll have to wait until you are almost at the summit before the view finally opens up. The highest point offers a terrific view south, but you'll probably want to continue heading east for a short distance to the slightly lower east summit, recognizable by the presence of a lone tree perched atop. Watch for a large cornice on the left that may render this short traverse too dangerous. Stay at the west summit if that's the case. The view from the east summit (GR302161, 2100 m) is slightly better because more of the scenery to the east and north is visible. Take in a very pleasant view of the Opal Range, parts of the Elk and Misty ranges, the immense Lower Kananaskis Lake with mounts Fox, Foch and Sarrail in the background, as well as the impressive First World War battleship group of mounts Indefatigable, Invincible and Warspite to the southwest. Return the same way.

### Waypoints

The following waypoints can be used to assist in navigation once you have gained some elevation. Remember that these waypoints have an accuracy of ±100 horizontal m and ±10 vertical m.

Waypoint 1: 291164, 1970 m
Waypoint 2: 294163, 2018 m
Waypoint 3: 296163, 2030 m
East summit: 302161, 2102 m

# 44 "LITTLE LAWSON PEAK"

(MAP 7, PAGE 317)

DIFFICULTY MOSTLY MODERATE WITH A FEW DIFFICULT SECTIONS JUST BEFORE THE SUMMIT

HAZARD MOSTLY LOW, BUT MODERATE FOR THE FINAL FEW HUNDRED METRES

MOUNTAIN HEIGHT 2370 M

ELEVATION GAIN 600 M

ROUND-TRIP DISTANCE APPROX. 8 KM

ROUND-TRIP TIME 6–8 HOURS

ADDITIONAL EQUIPMENT POSSIBLY CRAMPONS AND AN ICE AXE FOR THE UPPER RIDGE

MAPS 82 J/11 KANANASKIS LAKES, GEM TREK KANANASKIS LAKES

*For some seclusion and a great view of the Opal Range and Lower Kananaskis Lake, this minor peak at the end of Mount Lawson's long south ridge makes for a great day out. The approach and ascent are straightforward, but the final few hundred metres may be challenging in certain conditions.*

## DIRECTIONS

Park at the Peninsula turnoff, near the south end of Highway 742. Walk about 100 m north on the highway to the wide trail and snowshoe sign on the opposite side of the road. Hike or snowshoe this trail. Soon the objective becomes visible ahead of you, looking a little more intimidating than it really is. About 1 km along the trail an old wooden aqueduct appears on the left. Follow the trail to the end of the aqueduct.

Lying to the right of the end of the 'duct is the beginning of the long ridge of Mount Lawson (see photo opposite). Cross Kent Creek on the right and find the least steep route up to the ridge. Once on the ridge, routefinding is easy. Simply follow the ridge north. There are steeper sections, then more gently graded ones. Views are limited, but occasional openings in the trees to the right reveal what will soon be an excellent view of the striking peaks of the Opal Range.

Perseverance is the key as you continue up the ridge. The 600 m of elevation gain along 2 km of horizontal distance means you'll have to work for the prize at the top. About 2–3 hours up, the trees on the ridge start to thin and the terrain becomes rockier. At the same time, the drop down the east face increases. Stay away from the edge if cornices have formed. A few sections may require you to go left into the trees to avoid the ridge.

Although maps depict the first highpoint as being treeless, this is not the case. The true and treeless summit of Little Lawson is 500 m north of this false summit. To see the real views, you must make the true summit. This is where the route may take on a more serious nature, however, depending on snow conditions. Again, be very wary of cornices. Plummeting down the east face would be very, very bad!

One section of the ridge narrows considerably for a few metres. If necessary, take your snowshoes off here and proceed on foot, preferably with crampons and ice axe. Beyond this section another false summit is an easy walk away, and then another 100 m of easy terrain takes you to the true summit, at GR305211, 2370 m.

On a clear day the wintery view of the Opal Range is guaranteed to impress, as is the view south to Lower Kananaskis Lake and the peaks around it. Return the same way. The descent should be fast and wonderfully effortless.

ABOVE: LITTLE LAWSON. THE ROUTE FOLLOWS THE LEFT SKYLINE.
BELOW: THE END OF THE AQUEDUCT WHERE THE LONG SOUTH
RIDGE BEGINS.

# KANANASKIS LAKES TRAIL

*Although only two routes from this area are described in this book, there is a fair amount of potential for new snowshoeing routes along this road, especially around Upper Kananaskis Lake. Routes starting at Pocaterra and Elk Pass parking lots are not included in that statement. Groomed ski trails leave both lots, and snowshoers should stay away from those areas unless travel on one is absolutely imperative. There are plenty of other places where snowshoers can enjoy the stunning beauty of the Kananaskis Lakes.*

A VERY EARLY-SEASON ASCENT OF RAWSON RIDGE.
NOTE THAT THE LARCHES ARE STILL CHANGING.

# 45 RAWSON LAKE

(MAP 7, PAGE 317)

| |
|---|
| DIFFICULTY EASY |
| HAZARD LOW |
| LAKE HEIGHT 2025 M |
| ELEVATION GAIN 300 M |
| ROUND-TRIP DISTANCE 8 KM |
| ROUND-TRIP TIME 3–5 HOURS |
| MAPS 82 J/11 KANANASKIS LAKES, GEM TREK KANANASKIS LAKES |

*This small lake sits below the awe-inspiring northeast face of Mount Sarrail. A well-used trail goes all the way there. Gaining the ridge north of Rawson Lake (see page 245) grants you a great view of the considerably larger Kananaskis Lakes, but it is a far more serious trip than the one described below.*

## DIRECTIONS

Follow Kananaskis Lakes Trail to the Upper Kananaskis Lake parking lot. From there, start along the easy-to-follow trail that swings around the southeast end of Upper Kananaskis Lake and then parallels the south side. About 1 km along you'll cross a bridge that spans Sarrail Creek. Shortly after, a trail sign instructs you to leave the main trail and turn left (southwest) onto Rawson Lake Trail. Follow this trail for 2 km as it winds its way up treed slopes to Rawson Lake. Take some time to enjoy the tranquil beauty of this area. Provided the lake is sufficiently frozen, you can snowshoe across it to the southwest corner. Return the same way or continue the trip to include Rawson Ridge (see next trip).

MOUNT SARRAIL REFLECTED IN THE PLACID WATERS
OF RAWSON LAKE. PROBABLY NOT A GOOD TIME TO
ATTEMPT TO SNOWSHOE ACROSS THE LAKE!

# 46 RAWSON RIDGE

(MAP 7, PAGE 317)

| | |
|---|---|
| DIFFICULTY | DIFFICULT |
| HAZARD | HIGH |
| RIDGE HEIGHT | 2392 M, 2444 M TO THE SUMMIT |
| ELEVATION GAIN | 365 M FROM RAWSON LAKE |
| ROUND-TRIP DISTANCE | 12 KM |
| ROUND-TRIP TIME | 5–7 HOURS |
| ADDITIONAL EQUIPMENT | AVALANCHE GEAR |
| MAPS | 82 J/11 KANANASKIS LAKES, GEM TREK KANANASKIS LAKES |

*This trip picks up where the trip to Rawson Lake leaves off, and it should not be taken lightly. Avalanche potential is high, and very stable snow conditions are essential for a safe journey. Very early- or very late-season ascents are recommended. Whether you choose to go early or late, be extremely careful about snowshoeing across the lake. The view from the ridge is fantastic. For the ambitious, the highpoint of the ridge is possible but it involves some difficult scrambling.*

## DIRECTIONS

Follow the instructions to Rawson Lake (see page 243). There are three ways to get to the base of the ridge at the west end of the lake. Easiest of the three is the direct route right across the lake or the route that follows the north shore. Be sure the lake is sufficiently frozen. If it isn't, snowshoe all the way around the south side of the lake to the base.

The best route to the ridge goes up the treeless slope at the

far west end of the lake (**avalanche danger**). There is avalanche potential on this slope. A safer, but more tedious, route can be taken farther east, through the trees, if avalanches are a concern.

Upon reaching the ridge, take in a splendid view over the Kananaskis Lakes and then either return the same way or snowshoe east along the ridge. An impressive highpoint sits at the far east end of the ridge. If the ridge is snow-free, it is possible to scramble up to that summit by going up the left side of the rockband. The scrambling is difficult and exposed for a few moves. In the more likely event that the highpoint is covered in snow, snowshoe up to it and then head down the south-facing slopes back to the lake. Follow the shoreline back to the approach trail and out.

*OPPOSITE: ASCENT AND DESCENT ROUTES FOR RAWSON RIDGE, AS SEEN FROM THE RIDGE ON THE SOUTH SIDE OF RAWSON LAKE. SD=SCENIC, BUT MORE DANGEROUS ROUTE. SR=SAFE ROUTE THROUGH THE TREES. RR=RAWSON RIDGE. HP=HIGHPOINT OF THE RIDGE. BELOW: LOOKING EAST ALONG THE BEAUTIFUL RIDGE.*

# HIGHWAY 1: CANMORE TO LAKE LOUISE

*Surprisingly, the stretch of Highway 1 between Canmore and Lake Louise offers very little in the way of snowshoe routes. Unlike the Smith-Dorrien (742), you cannot pull over almost anywhere on the highway, get out and start snow-shoeing. Highway 1A may be a better bet for those wanting to explore the area.*

SCENERY ON LIPALIAN MOUNTAIN.

# 47 STONEY SQUAW MOUNTAIN

(MAP 8, PAGE 318)

| | |
|---|---|
| **DIFFICULTY** VERY EASY | |
| **HAZARD** LOW | |
| **MOUNTAIN HEIGHT** 1885 M | |
| **ELEVATION GAIN** 190 M | |
| **ROUND-TRIP DISTANCE** 4.4 KM | |
| **ROUND-TRIP TIME** 1.5–2.5 HOURS | |
| **MAPS** 82 O/04 BANFF, GEM TREK BANFF | |

*This is about as easy as an official peak gets. Save Stoney Squaw for days when the avalanche hazard is high or for days when time and/or energy are not in abundance. Views are limited, so don't expect to be blown away. Undoubtedly, your drive time to and from the peak will double or even triple the time you spend ascending and descending it. To make the most of your day, you can combine this ascent with one of a nearby peak/trip such as Tunnel Mountain (see page 251).*

## DIRECTIONS

Near Banff, take the Mount Norquay turnoff. Drive up the hairpin switchbacks, enjoying the fact that you are gaining a large chunk of the elevation in your car! Turn in to the Norquay parking area and park immediately at the trailhead sign to the right. This is a popular trail and so more than likely it will be packed down. If it is, you may choose to hike instead of snowshoe. In this case, it is unlikely you will need snowshoes for any portion of the trip, but take them along just in case.

The trail enters the trees immediately and stays there throughout. It meanders through the forest, changing direction frequently, but in general it heads southeast. Just before the summit it circles around the southeast side of the mountain and then proceeds up to the summit. Unfortunately, much of the summit view is blocked by trees, so don't go up expecting an earth-shattering panorama.

Either return the same way or make a pleasant loop route by continuing on the trail as it goes down the ridge toward the northwest. You'll lose elevation quite quickly before the trail starts to trend more to the left. A long section of flatter terrain that traverses the side of the mountain follows. After that you'll have to regain a little elevation. The trail suddenly pops out of the trees onto a wider trail. Turn left and follow this trail easily back to the Norquay ski resort and your vehicle.

# 48 TUNNEL MOUNTAIN

(MAP 8, PAGE 318)

| | |
|---|---|
| DIFFICULTY | EASY |
| HAZARD | LOW |
| MOUNTAIN HEIGHT | 1690 M |
| ELEVATION GAIN | 245 M |
| ROUND-TRIP DISTANCE | 4.6 KM |
| ROUND-TRIP TIME | 1.5–2.5 HOURS |
| MAPS | 82 O/04 BANFF, GEM TREK BANFF |

*This is an easy and stress-free trip that can be combined with Stoney Squaw Mountain. Of course, you have to drive between destinations. Tunnel Mountain is the twin peak to Stoney Squaw. They have a very similar elevation and orientation, and both sport impressively steep northeast faces. Tunnel Mountain's east side is home to several traditional climbing routes. The excellent trail to the summit is used year round. If the trail is unbroken, snowshoes may be necessary; otherwise, go on foot. Given the heavy traffic on the trail, icy sections may develop. In this case, spikes or other forms of crampons will help for better traction.*

## DIRECTIONS

The trailhead is on the east side of the town of Banff. From Banff Avenue, head southwest and turn left onto Moose Street. At the end of Moose Street turn right onto Grizzly Street and then left onto St. Julien Road. Take another left onto St. Julien Way and look for the lower trailhead on the left side of the road. For the upper trailhead, continue along St. Julien Way and make a sharp left onto Tunnel Mountain Drive, arriving at the obvious trailhead in a few hundred metres. If Tunnel Mountain Drive is fully open, the upper parking area will save you a little distance and elevation gain.

From the lower parking area, the obvious trail starts at the trailhead sign, gains a little elevation and goes left, and then, through a series of large switchbacks, gains the road above and the upper trailhead. The upper trailhead is marked with a big sign giving details about Tunnel Mountain and the trail. The instruction to "stay on the trail and avoid shortcuts" is one everybody should follow religiously, even in winter when damage to the environment is less pronounced.

Specific directions are unnecessary because the trail is very clear and easy to follow. The path winds its way up the mountain in a series of large, gently graded switchbacks. For the final section the trail turns north along the very steep northeast face. Don't go too near the edge. Also be aware that climbers do ascend this face. As a sign clearly points out, do not throw anything down that face. Metal railings provide some security, and you'll want to check out the views by the railings.

The summit is treed, but if you wander around a little, respectable views lie in most directions. Views of the northwest arm of Mount Rundle and the Fairholme Range to the east, and looking down on the Banff townsite in its entirety, will likely be the most interesting. A short descent to a lower plateau around the north side of the mountain opens up the view to the west and north a little more. Return the same way. Do not attempt any shortcuts down the west side of the peak.

# 49 PURPLE PEAK AND LIPALIAN MOUNTAIN

(MAP 9, PAGE 318)

| | |
|---|---|
| DIFFICULTY | MODERATE |
| HAZARD | MODERATE |
| MOUNTAIN HEIGHT | 2713 M |
| ELEVATION GAIN | 1000 M |
| ROUND-TRIP DISTANCE | 18 KM |
| ROUND-TRIP TIME | 9–12 HOURS |
| ADDITIONAL EQUIPMENT | AVALANCHE GEAR, CRAMPONS, ICE AXE |
| MAPS | 82 N/08 LAKE LOUISE, GEM TREK LAKE LOUISE AND YOHO |

*Lipalian Mountain sits southeast of the Lake Louise Ski Area. The resort ski-out makes easy work of the approach, but once you're off the trail the trip can be quite strenuous. The route described is different from those outlined in Chic Scott's* Summits and Icefields *(The Pumpkin Traverse) and Mike Potter's* Ridgewalks in the Canadian Rockies. *Scott's route also takes in several nearby summits and might be a little too ambitious for snowshoers. However, the suggestion here of ascending Purple Peak followed by Lipalian is a reasonable compromise. Awesome views on a clear day.*

## DIRECTIONS

Take the turnoff to the Lake Louise Ski Area and Mountain

Resort. Drive 1.6 km up the road and turn right, into the Fish Creek parking lot. There are two ways into the area from the parking lot: either up the resort ski-out or up Temple Road. The ski-out is probably the better choice, as vehicles routinely use Temple Road. Hike up the well-packed ski-out for about 4 km. Snowshoes will probably not be necessary here. If they are, you may want to go onto Temple Road, which starts just a few metres north of the turnoff to Fish Creek parking lot and is marked by a hiking sign.

About 4 km up the trail, cross the first major ski run (watch out for skiers) and continue up the trail for another kilometre or so, heading northeast. At approximately GR623005, 2100 m , the ascent valley sweeps in from the right. Take a sharp turn to the right (southeast) and start up the valley, taking the line of least resistance. You now have the south slopes of Redoubt Mountain on the left and unofficial "Wolverine Ridge" on your right. If the trail has not been broken, the next couple of hours could be very strenuous. Follow the valley southeast at a gentle grade. Eventually it turns south, passing Unity Peak to the east. Purple Peak is visible due south. Taking the easiest and safest line, make your way southwest to the col between Wolverine Ridge and Purple Peak. At the col, turn south and snowshoe to the summit of Purple Peak (GR636983, 2670 m).

The summit of Lipalian lies about 1 km west of Purple Peak and can be reached in a leisurely 45 minutes. Follow the obvious ridge, turn south and snowshoe to the summit (GR628977, 2713 m). The view west should impress you. Return the same way. **Do not** descend the north slopes of Lipalian directly to the Lake Louise ski lifts. The ski resort is presently trying to discourage people from ascending Lipalian from the top of the chairlift, as a big avalanche could reach inbound skiers.

On the way to Purple Peak (out of the photo at the left).
The summit of Lipalian is at the centre.

# YOHO NATIONAL PARK

There is a great deal of potential in Yoho National Park for interesting and exciting snowshoe routes. One of the highlights of the park is Emerald Lake and its sublime surroundings. Snowshoeing around the lake or attempting the more ambitious objective of Emerald Peak above the lake are both great ways to spend a day. The summits of Mount Field and Paget Peak are attainable on snowshoes, though both mountains have considerable avalanche risk.

A few minutes east of Yoho nestles world-famous Lake Louise. Presently there are no official snowshoe trails around the lake, but several summer trails have in recent years become popular as snowshoe routes during the winter months. Refer to Appendix D on page 337 for suggestions. Although not described in this book, our May 2003 snowshoe ascent of Mount Fairview was extremely memorable, with fantastic views and a wild Crazy Carpet ride down. Note that this is a very serious ascent with much **avalanche danger** and is recommended only in late spring.

An atmospheric view of the fantastic peaks that surround
Lake Louise, from the summit of Mount Fairview.

(MAP 10, PAGE 318)

| DIFFICULTY | DIFFICULT |
|---|---|
| HAZARD | HIGH |
| MOUNTAIN HEIGHT | 2566 M |
| ELEVATION GAIN | 1200 M |
| ROUND-TRIP DISTANCE | 9–11 KM |
| ROUND-TRIP TIME | 7–11 HOURS |
| ADDITIONAL EQUIPMENT | AVALANCHE GEAR, CRAMPONS, ICE AXE, POSSIBLY A ROPE AND SLINGS FOR THE SUMMIT RIDGE |
| MAPS | 82 N /07 GOLDEN, GEM LAKE LOUISE AND YOHO |

*Careful routefinding will allow you to get to the summit of this terrific little peak without putting yourself in too much avalanche danger. However, even the safest route has some objective hazards, and other routes are far more dangerous. Also, success or failure will largely be determined by the condition of the approach trail. If the snow is deep and the trail unbroken, you may have to downgrade to a less ambitious objective right off the bat. Snowshoeing around and/or on Emerald Lake makes for a fine trip in itself. Wait for very stable snow conditions and clear skies to ascend this "gem" of a peak.*

## DIRECTIONS

Drive west on the Trans-Canada. Just past Field, BC, turn right and follow the signs to Emerald Lake. Drive to the end of the road and park at the Emerald Lake parking lot. The Hamilton Lake trailhead is signed and starts at the southwest side of the parking area. Throughout its 6-km length, the trail to Hamilton Lake is, for the most part, easy to follow – it is simply the most prominent gap through the trees. However, it may not always be so obvious, especially if a previous track is not present. The general direction of travel is west and northwest, but large and small switchbacks abound.

The first point of interest along the trail is Hamilton Falls, about 1 km in. Depending on snow conditions, the falls can be reached in as little as 20 minutes or as much as a full hour. Beyond the falls the trail gets a little steeper. While it is not relentlessly steep, travel for the next 1–3 hours can be strenuous and tedious. A good portion of the 1200 vertical m of elevation will be gained here. Downgrading your objective to Hamilton Lake or the highpoint above the lake may become necessary.

### Safe route to the summit of Emerald Peak

The safest route to the summit of Emerald Peak gains the south ridge as soon as possible, leaving the trail around GR303993, approximately 1900 m. After an hour or two of travel from the falls, the trail starts to side-hill toward Hamilton Lake, eventually crossing a large and very obvious avalanche slope. If you reach this avalanche slope (GR298000, 2037 m) you have gone too far. Back up a few hundred metres and turn north into the trees. Though it may not be obvious, you are now on the south ridge. Pick the least steep and safest route of travel to treeline. The reward for the arduous approach is soon to come, as the views in all directions start to open up. Proceed north to the false summit at GR299007, 2516 m.

### Scenic but trickier route to the South Ridge

A more scenic, but slightly longer and far more dangerous route continues toward Hamilton Lake. Cross the avalanche slope mentioned in the safe route above (**obvious avalanche danger**) and continue side-sloping northwest. Another prominent avalanche slope, on the southwest side of Emerald Peak, is soon reached. If your goal, at this point, is to reach the shores of Hamilton Lake and nothing else, cross this avalanche slope without gaining any elevation and follow the trail, or routefind your way to the lake, about 700 m away. Take in the splendid view of Mount Carnarvon and then return the way you came.

The key to the Emerald Peak route is an excellent viewpoint/col on the southwest side of the mountain. The col is a worthwhile destination in itself if the prospects of completing the ascent are diminishing. Instead of crossing the second avalanche slope without gaining elevation, go across and up it, toward the obvious col above (**more obvious avalanche danger**). The terrain above you is ripe for avalanches, so use extreme discretion here. At the col (GR296004, 2214 m), soak in the outstanding view of Mount Carnarvon, with Hamilton Lake below, before deciding whether to continue or not.

The most dangerous section of the trip follows – getting onto the south ridge. This requires a dangerous traverse and then a steep ascent to the ridge (see photo opposite). The route is only possible when conditions are almost 100 per cent benign. The ascent slope is about 35° – very steep for snowshoes and perfect for avalanches. Switch to crampons and an ice axe if it makes you feel more comfortable.

When you are out onto the safer terrain of the south ridge, turn north and gain the false summit with relative ease (GR299007, 2516 m). The false summit is another excellent viewpoint and gives you a chance to consider the short but challenging ridge ascent to the summit.

### Up to the summit (for both routes)
If you choose to go on to the summit, you will more than likely want to remove your snowshoes here and complete the ascent on foot. Crampons and an ice axe are a very good idea and will

ABOVE: ROUTE TO THE SOUTH RIDGE. SS=STEEP SLOPES UP TO 35°.
BELOW: [A] VIEW FROM NEAR THE FALSE SUMMIT. FS=FALSE SUMMIT.
D=DANGEROUS AVALANCHE SLOPES. DC=DOWNCLIMB.

be mandatory in certain conditions. Some will find a short rope useful for a couple of sections.

For safety reasons, it is best to stick to the ridge throughout. Unless it is completely snow-free, **do not** venture out onto the west side of the ridge to circumvent the first obstacle (see photo A, page 261). An avalanche here would be very serious.

Gain the next highpoint, a short distance away (also photo A) and then downclimb to the next col. Snow conditions may dictate how easy or difficult this downclimb is. Continue up easier terrain until you arrive at an interesting section of rock pinnacles (see photo B above). The left side offers a decent route past these small pinnacles. Expect a couple of moderate scrambling moves. Beyond the pinnacles, the summit is a short distance away (GR298010, 2566 m).

Even with The Presidents blocking views to north, the summit panorama is still a magnificent one. The Goodsirs, snowy Mount Vaux and several other distinctive peaks can be seen to the SSE and SW, respectively. Cathedral Mountain and Mount Stephen dominate the view to the southeast. The nearby peak to the east is Wapta Mountain. Much of the Emerald Lake route up The Presidents is visible. A quick look and it should become obvious why the majority of parties choose the route via the Stanley Mitchell Hut to the summits of these statuesque mountains.

Two feasible options for descent exist. The safest route is definitely the way you came up. Undoubtedly, all those who achieve

[C] THE ALTERNATIVE DESCENT ROUTE. SD=STEEP, DESCENT SLOPES. HP=HIGHPOINT OF THE EAST RIDGE EXTENSION. W=WAPTA MOUNTAIN. S=MOUNT STEPHEN.

the summit will note the huge avalanche slope that goes almost directly down to Emerald Lake (see photo C, page 263). This is the second descent option and, if and *only if* the snow stability is good, definitely the route of choice. It cannot be stressed enough that this slope is a classic avalanche slope and it **will slide** given the right conditions. Extreme discretion and severe scrutiny of the snowpack and conditions are required.

If you choose to descend the slope, start by retracing your steps back down the ridge, past the rock pinnacles. Lose a little more elevation and look for the least steep route to your left (east). Pick your line and down you go (**avalanche danger**). Watch for cornices lining the ridge above you. Don't let your guard down when you reach the gentler terrain in the bowl below, either. Avalanche debris can often be found along the entire length of the slope.

This descent route does offer excellent opportunities for glissading and Crazy Carpeting. There is only one way to go, so routefinding shouldn't be an issue. Follow the slope into a drainage that trends to the left. You will soon reach Emerald Lake. Turn right and hike or snowshoe back to your vehicle, only a few hundred metres away.

### An extra ridge on the second descent route

For a little extra bang for your buck on descent, visiting the ridge to the east of Emerald Peak is an easy, though still **avalanche-prone**, affair (see photo C). After descending most of the way into the bowl to the east of the summit, trend left and side-slope over to the small col. Then ascend the gentle terrain of the ridge. Cornices on the east side will likely be huge, so stay well away from the edge. Follow the ridge to its highest point (GR304010, 2426 m) and then return the way you came, making your way back to the bowl below. Follow the remainder of the descent route described previously.

# HIGHWAY 93 SOUTH

*Snowshoeing opportunities along the south section of Highway 93 (reached at the Castle Junction turnoff) are fairly minimal. Except in places ravaged by the 2003 fire, the forest is heavy and difficult to negotiate. The excellent trail system on the west side of the road does offer some potential for exploration, but be prepared for an extremely long day to gain enough elevation to enjoy the scenery.*

DESCENDING MOUNT HAFFNER.

# 51 MOUNT HAFFNER

(MAP 11, PAGE 318)

DIFFICULTY MODERATE

HAZARD MODERATE

MOUNTAIN HEIGHT 2535 M

ELEVATION GAIN 1140 M

ROUND-TRIP DISTANCE 11 KM

ROUND-TRIP TIME 6.5–9 HOURS

ADDITIONAL EQUIPMENT AVALANCHE GEAR

MAPS 82 N/1 MOUNT GOODSIR,
GEM TREK KOOTENAY NATIONAL PARK

*Mount Haffner is generally a safe bet when avalanche conditions are high. There are a couple of suspect slopes, but they are very short and have gentle runouts. Nevertheless, take your avalanche gear. Wait until late winter or early spring to make an attempt, unless 7 hours of knee-deep post-holing is your thing!*

## DIRECTIONS

From the Castle Junction turnoff, drive south on Highway 93 to the parking area for Numa Falls. The summit of Haffner is not visible from the parking area. When facing the mountain, to the left is the southeast ridge of Vermilion Peak and the summit of "Haffner Senior" can be seen to the right. Between them lies Mount Haffner.

Cross the road and start through the trees and up the lower slopes. There are several steeper sections, where switchbacking may be necessary. Soon you'll reach an old road that runs parallel to the highway. Cross that road and continue up, heading northeast. Ascending through the burnt remains of the 2003 fire is a fascinating experience in itself – at least for the first hour!

Follow the line of least resistance up. The direction of the slopes trends more toward Vermilion Peak to the north than Haffner, so expect a fair dose of side-sloping higher up unless you veer more to the right as you ascend. That said, veering right will entail a few elevation losses and regains as well as steeper terrain. In the long run, sticking to the general lay of the land will be easier.

The ascent slopes are deceptively long. After a couple of hours you should see the lower section of Vermilion Peak's south ridge to your left. Keep going up until the summit block of Haffner appears to the right, through the trees. When it does, start heading more to the right toward the col between Vermilion and Haffner, at GR628669, 2210 m. This will entail going across the slopes as well as up them.

[A] THE UPPER SLOPES OF MOUNT HAFFNER, VISIBLE THROUGH THE CHARRED TREES. SV=SOUTH RIDGE OF VERMILION PEAK. H=SUMMIT OF HAFFNER.

From the col the ascent is relatively straightforward. The summit appears to be on the left but is actually at the right (see photo B below). Stay on or near the ridge for the safest route. You may need to traverse left to circumvent snow drifts. Be careful – going left puts you onto steeper terrain that could slide (**avalanche danger**). The summit lies at GR639666, 2535 m.

The view features some very impressive peaks. Mount Ball lies due east and Stanley Peak to the northeast. The wall of rock to the southwest is appropriately named "The Rockwall," Foster Peak being the tallest mountain of the range. The infamous Goodsirs stand tall and proud farther north. Return the same way. More direct routes back to the highway are possible, but in terms of routefinding, those will probably cause you more stress and energy than the effort warrants.

[B] THE ROUTE TO THE SUMMIT, AS SEEN FROM THE CONNECTING RIDGE BETWEEN MOUNT HAFFNER AND VERMILLION PEAK. S=SUMMIT.

# HIGHWAY 93 NORTH

Highway 93 north, also called the Icefields Parkway, is as breathtaking an area as you can find on this planet – especially when snow has covered the landscape. The highway weaves its way among innumerable, strikingly beautiful peaks and several expansive icefields, the most notable of which is the world-famous Columbia Icefield (see *Snowshoe Ascents on the Columbia Icefield, page 325*). Near the south end of the road sits the Wapta Icefield. This sheet of ice and the peaks upon it are very accessible to skiers and snowshoers (see *Snowshoe Ascents on the Wapta Icefield, page 321*).

The enormous potential for snowshoe routes along the road is somewhat limited by a lack of feasible areas to park. There are some pull-outs, but there are long stretches of road without any. The snow often piles up high on either side of the road, and parking in the shoulder lane is very dangerous. Have a backup plan in case finding a safe place to park is a problem. Also note that this road is not regularly plowed. Driving it can be very treacherous right after and for long periods of time after a snowfall. Visit the Alberta Motor Association's Road Report page, at www.ama.ab.ca/road-reports, to check the condition of the highway before setting out.

THE VAST SNOW SLOPES OF MOSQUITO MOUNTAIN.

# 52 "HECTOR SOUTH"

(MAP 12, PAGE 319)

> DIFFICULTY MODERATE VIA THE SOUTH RIDGE,
> DIFFICULT VIA THE WEST RIDGE
>
> HAZARD HIGH
>
> MOUNTAIN HEIGHT 2970 M
>
> ELEVATION GAIN 1170 M
>
> ROUND-TRIP DISTANCE 9 KM FOR THE WEST RIDGE;
> 10 KM FOR THE SOUTH RIDGE;
> ADD 7-9 KM FOR THE EXTENSIONS TO THE SOUTH
>
> ROUND-TRIP TIME 8-14 HOURS
>
> ADDITIONAL EQUIPMENT AVALANCHE GEAR,
> CRAMPONS, ICE AXE, ROPE AND SLINGS FOR THE
> WEST RIDGE
>
> MAPS 82 N/9 HECTOR LAKE,
> GEM TREK LAKE LOUISE AND YOHO AND BOW LAKE
> AND SASKATCHEWAN CROSSING

*At a respectable height of 2970 m, views from the summit of this peak are very rewarding, especially toward the south face of massive Mount Hector. There is no established trail, so breaking one will probably be strenuous. The quickest and most challenging route ascends the west ridge. The south ridge avoids any major difficulties but still requires some hands-on scrambling. Both routes expose you to potential avalanche slopes.*

## DIRECTIONS

There are two routes to the top of Hector South: the South Ridge Route and the West Ridge Route. The first route is easier.

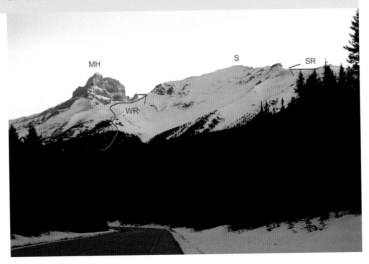

THE ROUTE AS SEEN FROM HIGHWAY 93, SEVERAL
KILOMETRES BEFORE YOU PARK. WR=WEST RIDGE.
SR=SOUTH RIDGE. S=SUMMIT. MH=MOUNT HECTOR.

# SOUTH RIDGE ROUTE

*Though much easier than the West Ridge Route, one rock-band en
route to the summit may stop some in their tracks. Crampons and
an ice axe may be useful for this step. If the upper ridge is prob-
lematic, you can salvage the day by going to a lower summit to the
southeast at GR540095, 2754 m.*

## DIRECTIONS

From Lake Louise, drive west and turn onto Highway 93 north.
Continue up the road for about 11.5 km and find a place to park.
If snow is piled high on both sides of the road, finding a safe
parking spot may not be possible. If that's the case, pick another objective (Cirque Peak or "Crystal Ridge," for example [see

pages 287 and 284]). If you do find parking, orient yourself to the northeast and away you go. The grade is gentle and the trees far apart. Nevertheless, considerable physical effort will be required to reach treeline, especially if the snow is unsupportive. There is a drainage to your right that you can use as a guide.

An hour, or even two, of strenuous travel should bring you to treeline and much better views. Keep going up and northeast, picking the least steep line. This may require you to trend a little to the right at one point, depending on where you came from. Eventually this route intersects the south ridge. Once you're on the ridge, turn north and follow it without difficulty at first. If the upper slopes are windblown you may decide to abandon your snowshoes and go on foot.

The pleasant hike to the summit is interrupted once by a steep-looking rock-band. Rather than tackle it head-on, circle around to the left (west) side and find the easiest way up. There is nothing terribly difficult here, but crampons and an ice axe may help if the terrain is snowy. Above the step, continue on easier terrain to the summit. Be very aware of the large cornices overhanging the east side and stay away from them.

When you reach the summit your effort will be amply rewarded with a fine view of Mount Hector. Return the same way. For optional visits to other highpoints along this interesting ridge, see the West Ridge Route descent description below. As stated, GR540095, 2754 m, to the southeast also makes a fine destination.

## WEST RIDGE ROUTE

*This route is for experienced snowshoers and scramblers only. The crux rock-band is steep and exposed, requiring an ice axe, crampons and solid scrambling skills. Some may even find it necessary to rope up here. If this doesn't sound good to you, use the easier South Ridge Route, noted above.*

From Lake Louise, drive west and turn onto Highway 93 north. Continue up the road for about 13 km and find a place to park. A small diamond-shaped red sign (GR499100) can be used as a guide. If this area is not clear of snow, pick another objective or drive back along the road and park as if you were following the South Ridge Route above, and then hike 1.5 km up the road to the starting point for this route. Remember, you must be parked completely off the road – parking in the shoulder lane is very dangerous.

The summit and ridge are visible a kilometre or two before the parking area. Be sure to take a look to see how much snow there is. Getting to the correct ascent ridge will probably involve a little hit and miss, as the ridge is not visible until you are actually on it. From the parking area, simply head into the trees and go up and northeast. The slope is generally not steep, but the condition of the snow will determine how strenuous this part of the ascent is. Deep, unconsolidated snow will give you the workout of your life! The slope is also much longer than you may think. Be prepared for the ascent to treeline to take 1.5–2 hours.

As the trees begin to thin out, the terrain will become steeper, some of it with avalanche potential (**avalanche danger**). Keep going up, taking the safest and easiest line. The goal is to gain the north-trending ridge that lies to the southwest of the summit, around GR513110. Depending on your route, you may end up at either end of this wide ridge or somewhere near the middle.

The remainder of the ascent is visible once you gain the ridge (see photo A opposite). Follow the ridge north and then east as it approaches the crux rock-band. Cornices in this area of the Rockies can grow to enormous sizes. Be wary of the cornice to your right and stay well clear of the edge. Make a thorough assessment of the rock-band before tackling it. If steep slopes on

the left side of the band are plastered in deep, unstable snow, your day may have just ended. Trade your snowshoes for an ice axe and crampons at this point. Some may wish to put on a harness and get out a rope and a few slings for protection. Strap your snowshoes to your pack, as you will likely choose the easier descent route, as opposed to coming back the same way.

The best route up the rock-band stays as close to the middle as possible. This, of course, is also the steepest route, and almost immediately you will encounter terrain that is fit for lower-fifth-class climbing. When this happens, traverse left on good ledges (probably snow-covered) and look for an easier ascent route, always trying to trend back to the centre. Repeat this procedure several times as you make your way up the band. The rock is generally very solid but there are some large loose blocks. Check all holds before committing to them. Again, don't be afraid to take out the rope if this terrain feels precarious. The rock offers decent belay stances and opportunities to place slings around boulders. Although trending far to the left will seem like a good idea it will also increase your exposure and risk of a fatal fall. Should the snow give way on these slopes you will have little to no time to arrest before plummeting down the face. A rope and good belay will make this entire section much less tenuous.

The first 40-odd metres of the rock-band are the toughest. Above that lies easier terrain, though caution is still warranted due to exposure and one particularly narrow section of the ridge. Past that you can finally breathe again and take in the terrific view of Mount Hector's imposing south face. Continue easily up to the summit. On a clear winter day, the summit view will not be a letdown.

If you're using GPS, the following GR coordinates will help you navigate the route:

510109, 2300 m – open area where the terrain gets steeper; the ridge is directly above

513110, 2470 m – the ridge

514117, 2670 m – nearing the crux rock-band

521119, 2970 m – the summit

The greatest challenge of the descent will be in deciding how much more work you are willing or capable of doing. The first and recommended option is to follow the ridge south for about a kilometre and then work your way down to the valley and then back up to your ascent tracks. The second, and most productive, option is to follow the winding ridge south to take in a couple of lower summits before working your way back to the highway, followed by a walk of several kilometres back to your car. This option is very physically taxing and will require more strenuous trail-breaking, though at least it will be downhill. The third option is to return the same the way you came. This is provided you are comfortable downclimbing or rappelling the crux rock-band. Of the three options, this last one is the least strenuous but the most difficult.

### Descent option one (recommended)

Simply follow the ridge south, again staying far away from the cornice to your left. A rock-band is soon encountered at GR522113, 2840 m, though is it far less serious than the rock-band on the west ridge. Descend the colourful band on its right (west) side. Continue along the ridge for a short distance and then turn west to a very minor highpoint. You should now be able to see the ridge you ascended across the valley. Getting to that ridge requires you to descend into the valley (**avalanche danger**) and then up the other side back to your tracks. These slopes don't appear to be too steep, but they are steep enough to avalanche. Use discretion. If unsure, return to the ridge and go further south to

THE VIEW SOUTH TO OTHER SUMMITS AND THE FIRST, AND EASIEST, DESCENT OPTION. GR1 GR540095. GR2 GR539073.

find gentler slopes. Following your ascent tracks down should be very fast and easy.

### Descent option two (longest)

For the second and longest descent option, use the same instructions as the option above, but once below the rock-band, continue heading south along the ridge. There are no difficulties beyond the rock-band. Keep going south, basically until you conk out! Escaping the ridge is generally straightforward at any point. Remember, you'll have to break trail back to the road. Those with Herculean endurance and quadriceps could possibly make it all the way to GR539073 before turning west toward the road. Perhaps more rewarding, however, is to turn southeast at approximately GR530097 and go to a summit at GR540095, 2754 m. Return back to GR530097 and then head for the road, taking the least steep route. If you complete this lengthy and very strenuous traverse you're a better man than I am!

THE IMPOSING SOUTH SIDE OF 3394 M MOUNT HECTOR,
AS SEEN FROM THE SUMMIT OF HECTOR SOUTH.

# 53 MOSQUITO MOUNTAIN

(MAP 12, PAGE 319)

| | |
|---|---|
| DIFFICULTY | DIFFICULT |
| HAZARD | HIGH |
| MOUNTAIN HEIGHT | 2970 M |
| ELEVATION GAIN | 1130 M |
| ROUND-TRIP DISTANCE | 18 KM |
| ROUND-TRIP TIME | 9–12 HOURS |
| ADDITIONAL EQUIPMENT | AVALANCHE GEAR |
| MAPS | 82 N/9 HECTOR LAKE, GEM TREK BOW LAKE AND SASKATCHEWAN CROSSING |

*The 6-km approach to the base of Mosquito Mountain is a very popular winter route for skiers and snowshoers. However, once you leave the hard-packed trail, expect anywhere from 500–1000 vertical m of strenuous trail-breaking through deep, unconsolidated snow. As such, a late-season ascent is recommended, when the snow may be more supportive. Mosquito Creek and Molar Pass's environs are superb and the ascent of Mosquito is outstanding. Nothing less than perfect weather will do here.*

## DIRECTIONS

Park at Mosquito Creek Campground on the west side of Highway 93 (north), about 24 km north of the junction with the Trans-Canada. Cross the road and find the trailhead by the northeast side of the bridge. This is a fairly popular trail in summer and winter. Hopefully, previously made tracks will make it easy to follow. The trail almost immediately ascends slopes to the left, making its way to the upper bench above Mosquito Creek. It soon turns north, paralleling the creek a fair distance away. This trail is generally wide enough to support separate ski and snowshoe trails, although they will be very close to one another.

The first 2 km of the trail stays in the trees. The trail then descends to the creek, where you'll find good views of the trio of Mosquito Mountain, The Ramp and Quartzite Peak. Note the potential ascent routes from here (see photo A below) Continue following the creek, mostly on its north and west bank, for another 4 km to the Mo 5 Campground. Expect to take 1.5–2 hours to get from the parking lot to the campground.

There are several routes to treeline from the campground. If the off-trail snow is supportive, Route 1 is recommended. If you sink past your knees upon leaving the trail, try Route 2 (see photo A).

### Route 1

From the campground, leave the trail (GR480241) and head into the forest, going northeast. Initially, you can more or less follow

[A] THE VIEW OF MOSQUITO MOUNTAIN AFTER DESCENDING TO THE CREEK. 1=ROUTE 1. 2=ROUTE 2. S=SUMMIT.

the creek for a short distance, but then you start heading up and to the left through the trees. The terrain gets steeper and will be very strenuous to ascend if the snow is not supportive.

At GR487250 the trees suddenly disappear and the remainder of the route comes into full view. Head up the open slopes until the left side of the mountain starts to fall away. At this point, the most scenic route goes over to the left and follows the vertiginous southwest ridge. Ascending slopes to the right is not recommended, because of avalanche potential. Also, some of the rock scenery to the left of the ridge is very interesting and shouldn't be missed. Of course, always be aware of cornices to the left.

### Route 2

This route is a little less steep than Route 1, but you should still expect it to be a strenuous affair. From the campground, stay on the trail. It immediately crosses over to the south side of Mosquito Creek and then parallels the creek, going east. Stay on the trail for about 1 km and then turn left (north) into the forest. Pick your way up the south slopes of Mosquito Mountain, taking the least steep route. One of several drainages may provide the best route, but be aware that sections of the drainage are terrain traps (**avalanche danger**). The slopes on either side of the drainage are steep enough to avalanche.

Persist up the treed slopes. The rewards of the open terrain above are well worth the considerable effort required to get there. When the trees do start to thin, look left for the easiest (and safest) route to the southwest ridge of the objective. This may require some minor elevation loss to avoid cutting across potential avalanche slopes. Good routefinding will minimize the danger. A direct route to the summit is not recommended, because of serious avalanche concerns.

When you reach the ridge, follow it northeast toward the summit, staying well clear of the huge cornice on the left side.

### To the summit (for both routes)

Follow the scenic southwest ridge. The views toward The Ramp are excellent. Soon, the right side of the mountain starts to fade away and the ridge narrows considerably, ending in a short drop-off. If conditions permit, downclimb on either side of the ridge to get past this obstacle. More than likely you will have to back up and escape to the east onto less exposed terrain. This will probably be the crux of the trip, and it does require stable snow conditions (**avalanche danger**) (see photo B). Circumvent the drop-off on fairly steep terrain and then return to the ridge as soon as possible. After the step, continue without difficulty to the summit at GR504263.

The summit panorama features the three peaks of Mount Willingdon to the northeast, as well as Cataract Peak farther south. To the south, the glaciated north face of Mount Hector is quite a spectacle. Molar Mountain and Noseeum Mountain are also prominent, as are the lengths of the Pipestone and Molar valleys.

Return the same way. There are plenty of glissading opportunities for those who brought their Crazy Carpets. Plunge-stepping down may be just as much fun.

[B] DESCENDING MOSQUITO MOUNTAIN. THE SNOW ARÊTE AT THE BOTTOM RIGHT IS THE CRUX STEP.

THE VIEW NORTH FROM THE SUMMIT, WITH THE RAMP AND QUARTZITE PEAK RECEIVING THE BRUNT OF THE SUN.

# 54 "CRYSTAL RIDGE"

(MAP 12, PAGE 319)

| | |
|---|---|
| DIFFICULTY | MODERATE |
| HAZARD | MODERATE |
| MOUNTAIN HEIGHT | 2600 M |
| ELEVATION GAIN | 640 M |
| ROUND-TRIP DISTANCE | 7 KM |
| ROUND-TRIP TIME | 5–7 HOURS |
| ADDITIONAL EQUIPMENT | AVALANCHE GEAR |
| MAPS | 82 N/9 HECTOR LAKE, GEM TREK BOW LAKE AND SASKATCHEWAN CROSSING |

*Unofficially named "Crystal Ridge" by Bob Spirko in 2001, this is a good alternative to Cirque Peak (see page 287). The summit is close to the road, and solid routefinding will help you avoid most of the objective hazards. Still, exposure to some avalanche terrain is unavoidable, and you should pack avalanche gear for this trip. Though not as stellar as those seen from Cirque Peak, the views from Crystal are still spectacular.*

## DIRECTIONS

Park near the trailhead in the Helen Lake parking lot. If the parking lot is inaccessible, you can also park at the Crowfoot pull-out, across the road. In general, the route to the ridge goes northeast. Start at the marked Helen Lake trailhead and snowshoe north up the trail, easily gaining elevation. Depending on how many travellers the route has seen previously, the path may be very easy to follow or a routefinding challenge. Keep going north on the trail for about 20 minutes. At around GR394240, approximately

ABOVE: Typical terrain above treeline on Crystal Ridge. (Photo by Bob Spirko)

BELOW: Heading to the summit. (Photo by Bob Spirko)

2050 m, the trail swings around to the east. Leave the trail (if in fact you were on it to begin with) and go northeast into the trees. The bush is light here and easy to negotiate.

Trend a little left as you gain elevation through the trees. If you go too far right you will end up on steeper, more open terrain that will definitely be avalanche-prone. Stay in the trees, continuing NNE. Expect some slightly steeper terrain along the way.

Above treeline the route should become fairly obvious. You are aiming for the low col that lies northwest of the objective at GR400254, 2542 m. Pick the least steep line to that col, assessing conditions as you go up. At the col, turn right (southeast) and snowshoe up to the summit, a few hundred metres away (GR401252, 2590 m). Enjoy the wonderful summit views.

Return the same way you came in. If you want to extend the day, however, there are two options.

### Extension to the southeast summit

A slightly lower summit lies about 800 m to the southeast and can be reached by just following the ridge to GR4062467, 2574 m. This traverse does put you on one steep slope and should be treated with caution. Also watch for cornices on the east side. The summit view is only marginally different from that of the true summit. However, the journey to the summit has several wonderful scenic opportunities and is well worth the effort.

### Extension to the northwest summit

Perhaps a better (and much safer) trip extension involves returning to the col and continuing northwest along the ridge for 600 m to the highpoint at GR399257, 2600 m. Again the summit view is not very different from that experienced on the true summit. Travel beyond the highpoint gets tricky and is only recommended for those who are comfortable on steeper terrain with increased avalanche hazard.

# 55 CIRQUE PEAK

(MAP 12, PAGE 319)

| | |
|---|---|
| **DIFFICULTY** DIFFICULT | |
| **HAZARD** HIGH | |
| **MOUNTAIN HEIGHT** 2993 M | |
| **ELEVATION GAIN** 1100 M | |
| **ROUND-TRIP DISTANCE** 15 KM | |
| **ROUND-TRIP TIME** 8–11 HOURS | |
| **ADDITIONAL EQUIPMENT** AVALANCHE GEAR, CRAMPONS, ICE AXE, POSSIBLY A ROPE AND SLINGS TO REACH THE TRUE SUMMIT | |
| **MAPS** 82 N/9 HECTOR LAKE, GEM TREK BOW LAKE AND SASKATCHEWAN CROSSING | |

*Winter or summer, Cirque Peak is an outstanding destination, offering a remarkable summit view. The trip is fairly long and has considerable objective hazards. Careful routefinding can steer you clear of some of those dangerous areas, but not all are avoidable. Crampons, an ice axe and possibly even a rope may be needed to reach the true summit. Late-season ascents are recommended.*

## DIRECTIONS

Drive north on Highway 93 for about 29 km and park at the small pull-off on the east (right) side of the road at the Helen Creek bridge (unmarked). The pull-off lies about 4 km north of Mosquito Creek Campground or 4 km south of the Helen Lake trailhead. The unofficial trail starts here, heading left and immediately up. This is a very popular winter trail and more than likely it will already be broken for skis and snowshoes. As usual, make a separate snowshoe trail if one does not exist.

After gaining a fair amount of elevation to reach the ridge above Helen Creek, the trail parallels the creek for a while and then drops down to it and crosses to its east side. Continue northwest, following the creek for about 1.5 km. The trail then crosses the creek that originates from Katherine Lake and begins to climb, a little to the right (north), through treed terrain.

When near treeline, trend more to the left so as not to gain the high ridge above. This ridge can be used as an ascent route, but you may want to save it for the return trip. Traverse open slopes well below this ridge toward Helen Lake (see photo A opposite). Continue going northwest until Helen Lake becomes visible. You will probably be on slopes that are a little higher than the lake. Snowshoe past the lake and then look for a feasible route up to the ridge to your right (east). There are rock-bands above; you'll want to be to the right (south) of them. This is the most potentially dangerous section of the trip (**avalanche danger**). Upon gaining the ridge, turn north and follow the south ridge of Cirque Peak toward the summit. The route is very obvious from here (see photo B).

The final ascent slope starts off gently but quickly rears up to more dangerous angles (**avalanche danger**). Crampons and an ice axe should replace your snowshoes well before the angle gets too steep. As always, assess avalanche potential as you gain elevation. A little scrambling is required to reach the false summit. The true summit is a short distance to the east. The traverse to the summit can be fairly intense in certain conditions because you must descend into a notch and then reascend to the summit. Some may feel the need for a rope and a belay. Stay at the false summit if the traverse looks iffy. If you choose to press on, a spectacular summit view will be the reward for your efforts. Dolomite Peak to the southeast and the Wapta Icefield due west are particularly striking from this vantage point.

Start the descent by returning to the point where you gained

ABOVE: [A] TRAVERSING SLOPES TOWARD HELEN LAKE.
CP=CIRQUE PEAK. BELOW: [B] THE OBVIOUS ROUTE UP
TO CIRQUE PEAK ONCE THE RIDGE IS GAINED.

Cirque Peak's south ridge. From here either return the same way you came or, for a little variety and more stellar views of Dolomite Peak, stay on the ridge, gaining a highpoint in short order. Continue following this ridge, going southeast, as it starts to gradually descend into the valley. Your ascent tracks are now below you to your right (west). Pick the least steep line trending right to rejoin those tracks and then snowshoe easily back to your vehicle.

TWO OF THE HIGHLIGHTS OF THE CIRQUE PEAK TRIP ARE THE UNIQUE AND WONDERFUL FORMS OF DOLOMITE PEAK (LEFT) AND MOUNT HECTOR (RIGHT).

| | |
|---|---|
| DIFFICULTY | DIFFICULT |
| HAZARD | HIGH |
| MOUNTAIN HEIGHT | 2670 M |
| ELEVATION GAIN APPROX. | 1400 M |
| ROUND-TRIP DISTANCE | 16 KM |
| ROUND-TRIP TIME | 10–12 HOURS |
| ADDITIONAL EQUIPMENT | AVALANCHE GEAR, CRAMPONS, ICE AXE |
| MAPS | 82 N/15 MISTAYA LAKE, GEM TREK BOW LAKE AND SASKATCHEWAN CROSSING |

*The price for a sensational view atop Survey Peak is several hours of body-numbing trail-breaking up heavily treed southeast slopes. Bring lots of friends to help share the trail-breaking duties, as well as avalanche gear, crampons and an ice axe for the upper slopes, not to mention a camera to capture the magnificent scenery. A late-season ascent may favour better snow conditions for the treed areas, but don't count on it! Given that the summer route to the top of this peak is same as this one, some may choose to save the ascent for a summer outing.*

## DIRECTIONS

Drive about 800 m west of the Saskatchewan River Crossing and turn left into the Glacier Lake Trail parking area. Begin at the far southwest end of the parking lot and follow the trail as it winds through light forest and then descends to the North Saskatchewan River. The trail is popular and should be easy to follow. Cross the river on a good bridge and continue along the trail, which now runs parallel to the wide Howse River. Though heavily treed on both sides, there are a few open areas that grant terrific views of mounts Murchison, Sarbach and Outram. Take advantage of them. One such area, just before the trail descends to Howse River, offers a good look at the ascent route and the large forested area you will have to contend with (see photo A opposite). Hopefully, that view will not deter you from the objective!

The trail eventually leaves the north side of Howse River and gradually ascends terrain southeast of Survey Peak, crossing a small stream several times on cut logs. It is possible to start ascending the peak anywhere is this general area – approximately GR135552, 5 km from the parking lot. Depending on how much time you've spent checking out the scenery, expect to take 1.5–2 hours to get to this point.

Leave the trail and start through the trees, heading NNW. The objective is to intercept the wide east ridge as soon as possible. The next few hours will test your group's stamina in a big way. Breaking trail upslope and through the trees will most likely be extremely strenuous. A solo ascent of this long slope would be a tremendous accomplishment.

The east ridge is not terribly distinctive. Look for the point at which the terrain flattens and starts to curve down to the north. An approximate GR reference to aim for would be 125564. When you're convinced you've reached the ridge, turn left and ascend the treed ridge going due west. If you've made it this far, persevere through more treed terrain. The payoff upon clearing the trees is a big one. Above treeline is a good place to rest, take in fantastic views of mounts Wilson, Murchison, Sarbach and Outram and contemplate the final 400 vertical m.

Continue up the ridge to another impressive view, this time of Survey's steep northeast face. At this point, it is advisable to trade your snowshoes for crampons and an ice axe and turn your avalanche beacons on. The final ascent slope is not terribly steep, but it is steep enough to slide. From the summit, the view of the complex massif of Mount Erasmus is another treat.

Return the same way you came in. Following your own tracks back will be very easy. Don't be tempted to try a more direct route to Glacier Lake Trail by travelling southeast from the summit. There are unseen steep sections of terrain in that direction.

ABOVE: [A] THE APPROXIMATE ASCENT ROUTE. S=SUMMIT.
BELOW: [B] R–L: FERENC JASCO, DAN COTE AND DREW NUG
APPROACHING THE SUMMIT BLOCK. THE SLOPES OF THE BLOCK
ARE MUCH STEEPER THAN THEY APPEAR IN THIS PHOTO.

# THE VALLEY NORTH OF MOUNT SASKATCHEWAN

The beautiful valley north of Mount Saskatchewan, a worthwhile destination in itself, is also the gateway to several fantastic unofficially named summits: "Big Bend Peak," "Mount Saskatchewan Junior," "The North Towers of Mount Saskatchewan" and "Spine Peak." The view from each of these peaks is outstanding.

If the trail through the trees up to the valley has not been broken, be prepared for a strenuous trek into the valley. Once there, enjoy terrific scenery as you head south toward the awe-inspiring form of 3342-m Mount Saskatchewan. Although the routes described in this section all avoid glaciers, the terrain around Mount Saskatchewan is heavily glaciated – take the proper precautions if travelling in that area.

If winter camping is your thing, this valley is a great location in which to spend a few days. Just watch where you camp – many areas sit at the bottom of avalanche slopes. Snow persists well into May and often into June here. This being so, you may want to wait patiently for a high-pressure system to roll into the area and then make your trip. Although the phrase "wait for a clear day" may appear far too frequently in this book, for the trips below, I really mean it!

ABOVE: Mark sits on the summit ridge of
The North Towers of Mount Saskatchewan.
BELOW: In the valley with Mount Saskatchewan ahead.

# 57 "BIG BEND PEAK"

(MAP 14, PAGE 320)

DIFFICULTY DIFFICULT VIA NORTHEAST RIDGE
HAZARD HIGH
MOUNTAIN HEIGHT 2814 M
ELEVATION GAIN 1100 M
ROUND-TRIP DISTANCE 10.5 KM
ROUND-TRIP TIME 8–11 HOURS
ADDITIONAL EQUIPMENT AVALANCHE GEAR,
POSSIBLY CRAMPONS AND ICE AXE
MAPS 82 C/3 COLUMBIA ICEFIELD,
GEM TREK LAKE COLUMBIA ICEFIELD

*This is the easiest ascent in the area and a terrific introduction to this part of the Canadian Rockies. Still, it's definitely a trip for the experienced snowshoer with avalanche training.*

## DIRECTIONS

Park in a large parking area at the west side of the "bend" of The Big Bend. Much of the route is visible from the parking lot – take a good look to the southwest and trace your route (see photo A opposite). The first order of business is to cross the North Saskatchewan River, about 100 m west of the parking lot. Thankfully, the river is quite narrow at this point and usually a good snow bridge spans the waterway. Later in the season the bridge may not be there. If this is the case, do the following: drive about 1 km east from where you've parked and turn right onto an unmarked gravel road. Walk across the bridge that spans a small but scenic canyon. Hike or snowshoe along the south bank of the river until you are west of the Big Bend parking lot. The directions for both of these start points are the same from here.

Head west toward the trees to where a wide trail enters the forest. The trail turns left and then winds its way up the forested slopes. Snowshoe up the trail for about 20–30 minutes to the point where it starts to drop down into the North Saskatchewan River valley. Don't go down into the valley. Instead, turn 90° left and head southeast into the forest. The goal is to gain the treed ridge high above. To the right (southwest), gaps in the trees will afford occasional glimpses of a steep rock face. Use these quick looks to plan your ascent; you'll want to stay to the east of the face and then eventually end up above it. The terrain to the ridge gets fairly steep in places and making switchbacks is a good idea. You'll at least be happy you are gaining elevation, and some terrific views are soon to come.

It's decision time when you reach the ridge: a sharp right takes you up Big Bend; going left takes you down into the valley

[A] BB=ROUTE TO BIG BEND. O=ROUTE TO ALL OTHERS IN THE VALLEY. RF=ROCK FACE. FS=FALSE SUMMIT. THE ROUTE INDICATED THROUGH THE FOREST IS APPROXIMATE.

and several other objectives. For Big Bend, look to the right and, hopefully, you will see the snowy lower slopes of the northeast ridge through the trees. Start heading in that direction – southwest. For the next 1.5 km, the travelling through the trees can be tedious, but it is generally easy and too not steep.

Once you're out of the trees, routefinding will not be an issue. Follow the wide ridge southwest toward the false summit at approximately GR933782, 2600 m. The grade now steepens and you should turn on your avalanche beacons. The steepest and most dangerous part of the ascent occurs near the beginning (**avalanche danger**). The grade eases a little as you approach the false summit.

From the false summit the remainder of the ascent is clear. This viewpoint will provide one of best vistas of the day – the summit block of Big Bend, half in sun and half in shadow (see photo B). When you've finished gawking at this marvellous sight, resume the ascent, losing a little elevation and then following the beautiful ridge to the top. Crampons and ice axe will probably not be necessary, but I would have them in my pack just in case.

Although great views of mounts Athabasca and Andromeda have been your companions throughout the ascent, it is not until you reach the summit that other giants make their appearances. If the more distant forms of Mount Columbia and Mount Bryce

don't impress you, the much closer Mount Saskatchewan massif is bound to do the trick. The summit of Big Bend is also a good vantage point from which to check out additional ascents in the area. The routes up Mount Saskatchewan Junior and The North Towers of Mount Saskatchewan are visible. Return the same way.

ABOVE: [B] THE TERRIFIC VIEW OF BIG BEND PEAK FROM THE FALSE SUMMIT. THE NORTH TOWERS OF MOUNT SASKATCHEWAN ARE ON THE LEFT OF BIG BEND. BELOW: [C] PART OF THE SUMMIT VIEW. S=MOUNT SASKATCHEWAN, NTS=THE NORTH TOWERS OF MOUNT SASKATCHEWAN, B=MOUNT BRYCE, MSJ=MOUNT SASKATCHEWAN JUNIOR, C=CASTLEGUARD MOUNTAIN, MC=MOUNT COLUMBIA, AN=MOUNT ANDROMEDA, AT=MOUNT ATHABASCA.

# 58 "SPINE PEAK"

(MAP 14, PAGE 320)

DIFFICULTY DIFFICULT VIA WEST SLOPES AND NORTH RIDGE, MOUNTAINEERING

HAZARD HIGH

MOUNTAIN HEIGHT APPROX. 2920 M

ELEVATION GAIN APPROX. 1200 M

ROUND-TRIP DISTANCE 15 KM

ROUND-TRIP TIME 9-12 HOURS

ADDITIONAL EQUIPMENT AVALANCHE GEAR, CRAMPONS, ICE AXE, POSSIBLY ROPE AND A FEW SLINGS FOR THE SUMMIT BLOCK

MAPS 82 C/3 COLUMBIA ICEFIELD, GEM TREK LAKE COLUMBIA ICEFIELD

*When viewed from certain angles "Spine Peak" resembles the spine of an alligator. Due to its strategic location relative to Mount Saskatchewan, the summit view is fantastic. This is a very serious ascent that goes up several avalanche slopes. It will probably appeal only to hardcore snowshoe mountaineering types. Winter ascents are strongly discouraged. Wait until April or May, or even do the ascent in September or October, when avalanches are less likely.*

## DIRECTIONS

The start of the approach is the same as it is for "Big Bend Peak" (see page 296).

Park in large parking area at the west side of the "bend" of The Big Bend. Much of the route is visible from the parking lot – take a good look to the southwest and trace your route (see photo on page 297). The first order of business is to cross the North Saskatchewan River about 100 m west of the parking lot. Thankfully, the river is quite narrow at this point and usually a good snow bridge spans the waterway. Later in the season the bridge may not be there. If this is the case, do the following: drive about 1 km east from where you've parked and turn right onto an unmarked gravel road. Walk across the bridge that spans a small but scenic canyon. Hike or snowshoe along the south bank of the river until you are west of the Big Bend parking lot. The directions for both of these start points are the same from here.

Head west toward the trees to where a wide trail enters the forest. The trail turns left and then winds its way up the forested slopes. Snowshoe up the trail for about 20–30 minutes to the point where it starts to drop down into the North Saskatchewan River valley. Don't go down into the valley. Instead, turn 90° left and head southeast into the forest. The goal is to gain the treed ridge high above. To the right (southwest), gaps in the trees will afford occasional glimpses of a steep rock face. Use these quick looks to plan your ascent; you'll want to stay to the east of the face and then eventually end up above it. The terrain to the ridge gets fairly steep in places and making switchbacks is a good idea. You'll at least be happy you are gaining elevation, and some terrific views are soon to come.

It's decision time when you reach the ridge: a sharp right takes you up Big Bend; going left takes you down into the valley and several other objectives. At this point go left, descending easy, treed slopes. You can start veering to the right almost immediately as you lose elevation into the valley. Trend sharply to the right and slightly down. If you lose elevation too fast you may end up high above the steep canyon wall of the drainage and then have to backtrack.

Within minutes, you should arrive at the start of the beautiful valley that eventually leads to Mount Saskatchewan's awesome north face. A creek bisects the valley and you can follow it south toward the base of Spine Peak and other objectives in the area. Initially, travel is easiest on the left (east) side of the creek. Bypass two scenic, canyon-like features, again on the east side of the creek. Beyond the second canyon you will see heavily treed terrain ahead. You'll want to cross to the west side of the creek as you approach the trees.

The crux of the approach is now upon you. The creek becomes difficult to follow, so you must gain elevation on the right (west) side of the creek and then resume travelling south, through the trees. There is nothing too difficult here, but trail-breaking may be strenuous and routefinding tedious. Persevere through this section and then descend back to the creek when the trees start to thin.

Once back at the creek, continue up the valley for about 15–20 minutes, looking to your left for the ascent route up Spine Peak. The route goes between the two prominent peaks directly above you to the east. The one on the right is Spine Peak and to the left sits Spine's northern outlier (see photo A opposite).

For the next several hours you will be exposed to some fairly serious avalanche terrain (**avalanche danger**). Proceed only if you are confident that conditions are stable. Turn east and head upslope, picking the least steep, and safest, line. Upon reaching the first bench, trend more to the left and up toward the gap between the two peaks. Ascend more avalanche slopes up to the second bench, where most of the remainder of the route is clear (see photo B). The red-lined route on the photo is by no means the only route to the ridge, but it is the least steep. Even so, the grade throughout is in the avalanche range. Pick the safest line possible, which means staying away from the very dangerous area on the northwest side of Spine Peak. If a line of bare rock is exposed, it may provide a steeper but safer route.

Upon reaching the ridge, trade snowshoes for crampons and an ice axe and proceed south, up the north ridge. This ridge gets fairly steep for the final push to the false summit. Most parties will go unroped, but some may want the security of a belay at distinctive rock-band a few metres from the false summit. The true summit is a short ridgewalk away. It is not deathly exposed but may feel that way if cornices remain and/or the snow is piled high and narrowly. If this short traverse looks spooky, stay at the false summit – the view is just as good here as it is at the top.

Needless to say, the summit view of Mount Saskatchewan is impressive, as are the distinctive pinnacle formations on Saskatchewan's east flank. Farther east and north sits another massive mountain, Mount Amery. Like Saskatchewan, Amery comes very close to the 11,000-ft. (3353-m) mark, falling a mere 79 ft. (24 m) short. Its glaciated summit plateau is gorgeous. To the

[A] IN THE CREEK, LOOKING LEFT (SOUTHEAST) TOWARD SPINE PEAK. SP=SPINE PEAK. O=OUTLIER TO THE NORTH.

right of Saskatchewan, Mount Bryce takes on a very different look than one normally sees from peaks farther north on the Columbia Icefield, and still farther right Mount Columbia asserts its superior height to all those that surround it. Return the same way you came in. You may chose to leave crampons on your feet for most of the upper slopes and then go back to snowshoes when the angle eases.

ABOVE: [B] D=DANGEROUS AVALANCHE SLOPES. THE ROUTE MAY VARY, DEPENDING ON CONDITIONS. BELOW: CHECKING OUT THE FINAL ASCENT SLOPE OF MOUNT SASKATCHEWAN JUNIOR.

# 59 "MOUNT SASKATCHEWAN JUNIOR"

(MAP 14, PAGE 320)

DIFFICULTY DIFFICULT VIA EAST RIDGE

HAZARD HIGH

MOUNTAIN HEIGHT 2850 M

ELEVATION GAIN 1150 M

ROUND-TRIP DISTANCE APPROX. 18 KM

ROUND-TRIP TIME 11–14 HOURS

ADDITIONAL EQUIPMENT AVALANCHE GEAR, CRAMPONS, ICE AXE

MAPS 82 C/3 COLUMBIA ICEFIELD, GEM TREK LAKE COLUMBIA ICEFIELD

*The unofficial title of the peak is perhaps something of a misnomer, given that "Junior" is quite distant from Mount Saskatchewan. However, the name (provided by Raff Kazmierczak in 2009) has stuck over the past few years. This is a very long and physically demanding day trip for those who wish to complete it as such. Leave early with a headlamp and plenty of food, water and sunscreen.*

## DIRECTIONS

The start of the approach is the same as it is for "Big Bend Peak" (see page 296).

Park in a large parking area at the west side of the "bend" of The Big Bend. Much of the route is visible from the parking lot – take a good look to the southwest and trace your route (see photo on page 297). The first order of business is to cross the North Saskatchewan River, about 100 m west of the parking lot. Thankfully, the river is quite narrow at this point and usually a good snow bridge spans the waterway. Later in the season the bridge may not be there. If this is the case, do the following: drive about 1 km east from where you've parked and turn right onto an unmarked gravel road. Walk across the bridge that spans a small but scenic canyon. Hike or snowshoe along the south bank of the river until you are west of the Big Bend parking lot. The directions for both of these start points are the same from here.

Head west toward the trees to where a wide trail enters the forest. The trail turns left and then winds its way up the forested slopes. Snowshoe up the trail for about 20–30 minutes to the point where it starts to drop down into the North Saskatchewan River valley. Don't go down into the valley. Instead, turn 90° left and head southeast into the forest. The goal is to gain the treed ridge high above. To the right (southwest), gaps in the trees will afford occasional glimpses of a steep rock face. Use these quick looks to plan your ascent; you'll want to stay to the east of the face and then eventually end up above it. The terrain to the ridge gets fairly steep in places, and making switchbacks is a good idea. You'll at least be happy you are gaining elevation, and some terrific views are soon to come.

It's decision time when you reach the ridge: a sharp right takes you up Big Bend; going left takes you down into the valley and several other objectives. At this point go left, descending easy, treed slopes. You can start veering to the right almost immediately after you lose elevation into the valley. Trend sharply to the right and slightly down. If you lose elevation too fast you may end up high above the steep canyon wall of the drainage and then have to backtrack.

Within minutes, you should arrive at the start of the beautiful valley that eventually leads to Mount Saskatchewan's awesome north face. A creek bisects the valley, and you can follow it south toward the base of Spine Peak and other objectives in the area. Initially, travel is easiest on the left (east) side of the creek. Bypass two scenic, canyon-like features, again on the east side of the creek. Beyond the second canyon, you will see heavily treed terrain ahead. You'll want to cross to the west side of the creek as you approach the trees.

The crux of the approach is now upon you. The creek becomes difficult to follow and so you must gain elevation on the right (west) side of the creek and then resume travel south, through the trees. There is nothing too difficult here, but trail-breaking may be strenuous and routefinding tedious. Persevere through this section and then descend back to the creek when the trees start to thin.

Back at the creek keep heading south. You are now about 3 km due east of the objective. However, before you start travelling in that direction, you have to get around the cliff faces to your right. Keep going up the valley until an obvious line to the right becomes visible. Turn right (west) and ascend slopes, trending a little north as you go. A 2-km stretch going WNW now takes you to the south side of Saskatchewan Junior's east ridge.

Gain the ridge when it seems easiest and follow it west toward the objective. The views of The North Towers of Mount Saskatchewan and Mount Saskatchewan itself are awesome throughout this section of the trip. Only the final section of the summit block will present a challenge. It does get steep and could slide (**avalanche danger**). Crampons and an ice axe may feel better than snowshoes do here. Take plenty of time to absorb the breathtaking summit view before deciding on your next course of action.

The overwhelming majority of parties will return the same way they came in at this point. If the nearby North Towers of Mount Saskatchewan looks tempting (and it certainly did to my

ABOVE: TYPICAL TERRAIN ON THE WAY TO THE "JUNIOR." SNOWSHOES WERE UNNECESSARY FOR THIS MAY ASCENT, BUT THEY REALLY CAME IN HANDY LATER IN THE DAY, ON DESCENT. MSJ=MOUNT SASKATCHEWAN JUNIOR. BELOW: THE SUMMIT VIEW FROM MOUNT SASKATCHEWAN JUNIOR. 11,000ERS MOUNTS ANDROMEDA AND ATHABASCA ON THE HORIZON (MARK MUST HAVE FLICKED THE ROPE, BECAUSE IT WAS A WINDLESS DAY),

brother and me), contemplate what you are in for if you make the attempt, and then go to the next trip.

# 60 "THE NORTH TOWERS OF MOUNT SASKATCHEWAN"

(MAP 14, PAGE 320)

DIFFICULTY DIFFICULT VIA NORTH RIDGE, MOUNTAINEERING

HAZARD HIGH

MOUNTAIN HEIGHT 2970 M

ELEVATION GAIN 1300 M

ROUND-TRIP DISTANCE APPROX. 22 KM

ROUND-TRIP TIME 15–18 HOURS (RECOMMENDED AS A TWO-DAY TRIP)

ADDITIONAL EQUIPMENT AVALANCHE GEAR, CRAMPONS, ICE AXE, ROPE AND A FEW SLINGS FOR SUMMIT RIDGE

MAPS 82 C/3 COLUMBIA ICEFIELD, GEM TREK LAKE COLUMBIA ICEFIELD

*This trip is the crowning achievement of those described in this section of the book. Views and scenery throughout are simply stupendous and the summit ridge and view are astounding. By late April to early May the snow may be supportive enough that much of the trip can be completed on foot. However, snow becomes isothermal pretty quickly in the May heat, and therefore snowshoes should be carried throughout the trip in case you need them.*

*The safest but longest route up avoids glacier travel by first ascending Mount Saskatchewan Junior, then proceeding due south to The North Towers. As a day trip, this endeavour will put your physical stamina to the ultimate test. If travel conditions are easy, expect to take at least 15 hours for the round trip. If travel conditions are not easy, don't even bother – do it as a two-day trip. The narrow summit ridge may not be negotiable, even with a rope and protection. Even if this is the case, you'll only miss the summit by a few vertical metres, and you will still be treated to amazing views.*

## DIRECTIONS

Follow the instructions for Mount Saskatchewan Junior (see page 305). From the summit, almost the entire route up The North Towers is visible, so a detailed description is unnecessary. Lose elevation easily to the col and continue south to the north ridge of The North Towers. Leave your snowshoes here at the base of the ridge and start up, on foot or with crampons (recommended) and an ice axe. Follow the ridge up to the first prominent rockband. There are several weaknesses in the band around the right side. Pick the easiest line (a few moves of difficult scrambling), and up you go. At the top, resume the scenic ridge ascent negotiating steeper terrain by traversing a little to the right or tackling it head-on.

Eventually you'll arrive at the false summit and the summit ridge. Even here the view is remarkable, and you should be content to call it a day if the remainder of the ascent gives you problems. The ridge is narrow, exposed and likely to be lined with a significant cornice. It may be very difficult to discern whether there's solid rock beneath the snow or just air. If you brought along a rope and some protection, finding good anchors may also prove to be an exercise in futility. Go as far as you feel comfortable and then stop to revel in the fantastic view. When satiated, return the same way. If you are doing this as a day trip, prepare yourself for perhaps one of the most physically and mentally numbing descents possible. Rest often and stay hydrated and nourished.

On the fantastic connecting ridge between Mount Saskatchewan Junior and The North Towers of Mount Saskatchewan. Note the avalanche debris at the lower left. MS=Mount Saskatchewan. NT=North Towers.

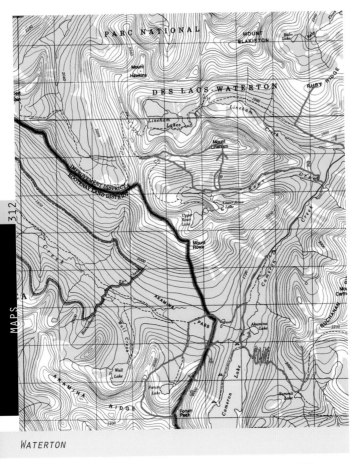

WATERTON

*Map 1*

HIGHWAY 774 CASTLE CROWN 1

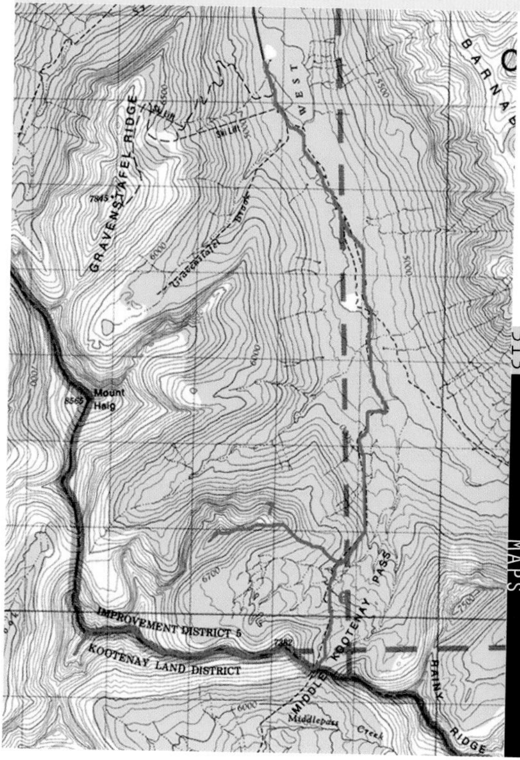


*Map 2*

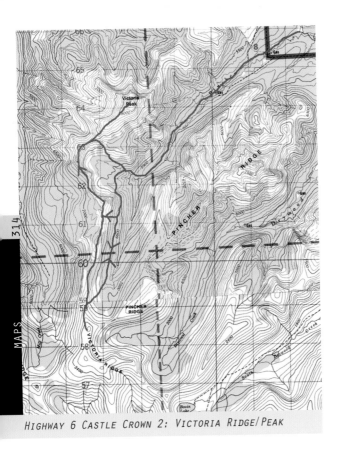

MAPS

HIGHWAY 6 CASTLE CROWN 2: VICTORIA RIDGE/PEAK

*Map 3*

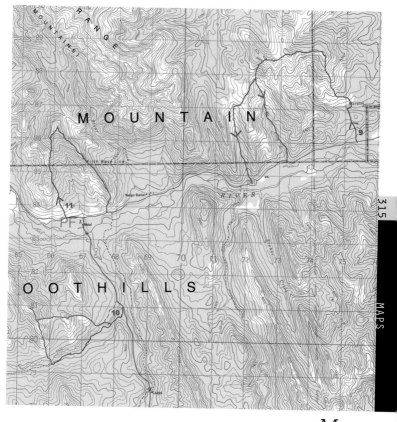

*Map 4*

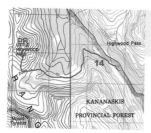

ABOVE: HIGHWAY 541
LEFT: HIGHWOOD: POCATERRA RIDGE

*Map 5*

# Map 6

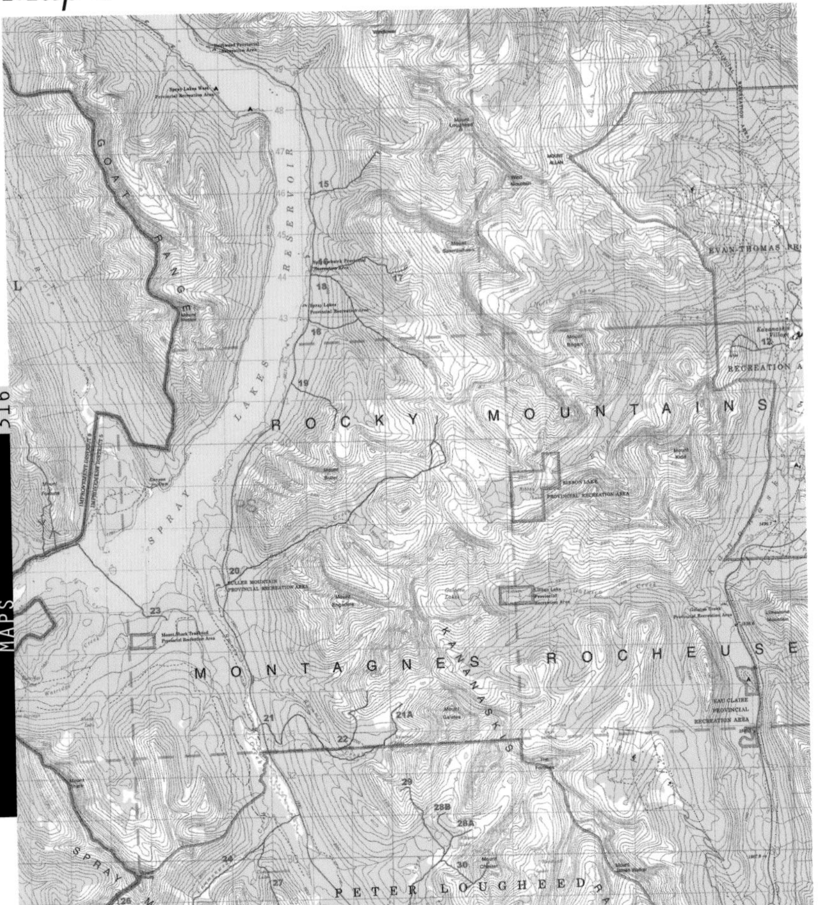

KANANASKIS NORTH

*Map 7*

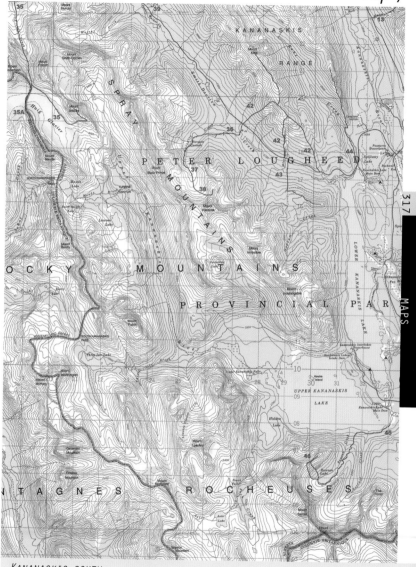

KANANASKIS SOUTH

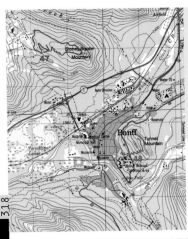

LEFT: Banff
MIDDLE: Lake Louise:
Lipalian Mountain
BOTTOM LEFT: Yoho: Emerald Peak
BOTTOM RIGHT: Kootenay:
Mount Haffner

*Map 8*

*Map 9*

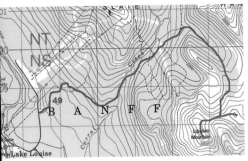

*Map 11*

*Map 10*

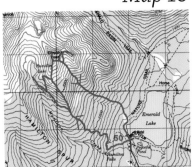

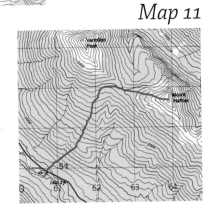

*Map* 12

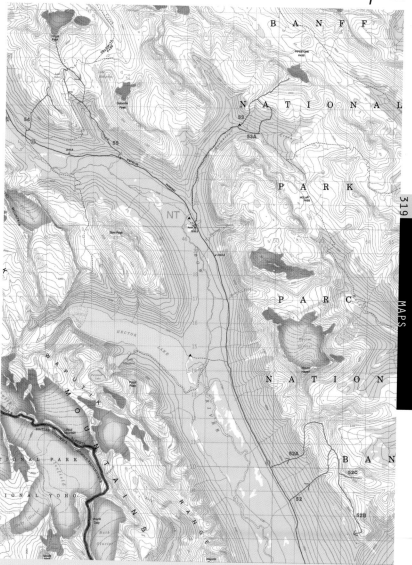

HIGHWAY 93 NORTH (SOUTH SECTION)

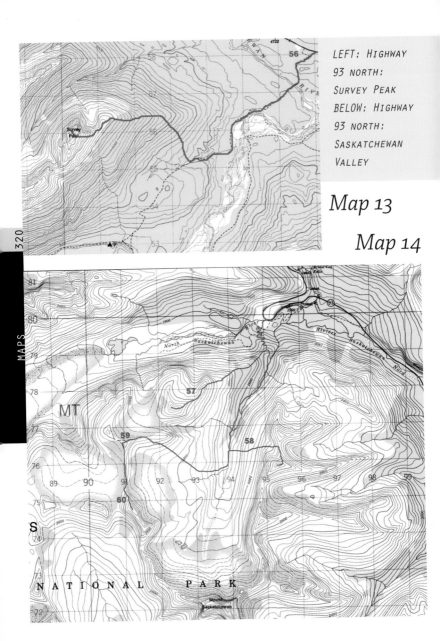

MAPS

LEFT: HIGHWAY
93 NORTH:
SURVEY PEAK
BELOW: HIGHWAY
93 NORTH:
SASKATCHEWAN
VALLEY

*Map 13*

*Map 14*

# Appendix A: Snowshoeing on the Wapta and Columbia Icefields

## Snowshoe Ascents on the Wapta Icefield

The Wapta Icefield is home to numerous beautiful peaks that are sometimes ascended on foot during the summer but more often on skis in the winter. Of course, that means that many of them are perfect for snowshoes, too. Several huts in the area, specifically the Bow Hut, provide perfectly situated bases where you can hang out for a couple of days while bagging peaks.

DESCENDING THE SLOPES ABOVE THE BOW HUT AFTER AN ASCENT OF MOUNT ST. NICHOLAS. SNOWSHOES WERE UNNECESSARY ON THIS EARLY DAY IN JANUARY.

There are a couple of items you should be aware of before you head to the Wapta Icefields. First, the Wapta has historically been the domain of backcountry skiers. It is very important that snowshoers be considerate about trail-breaking and the right of way. For most of the approach to the Bow Hut, for example, there is plenty of room to create a ski trail and a separate snowshoe trail. If no snowshoe trail exists, expend the energy to make one. Snowshoers who follow in your footsteps and skiers whose trail isn't pockmarked with snowshoe tracks will both be grateful. Once the trail is made it will be easy to reinforce when more snow comes. There is only one place – in the canyon – where snowshoers and skiers may need to share the same trail.

Skiers often travel slightly faster than snowshoers going uphill and infinitely faster downhill. Always yield the right of way to parties travelling at greater speeds no matter what their mode of transportation. Also be aware that skiers may be coming down through the treed sections of the approach, again at great speeds. Stay close to the edge of any trail and make yourself visible and/or audible to any oncoming traffic.

Each of the ascents described here can be completed as a day trip, but almost without exception they will push your physical stamina to its max. Be prepared for a minimum 10-hour (but sometimes 12–15-hour) day for most of the trips. If that timeframe doesn't appeal to you, book one of the huts with the Alpine Club at (403) 678 3200 or info@AlpineClubofCanada.ca.

Because all ascents below are described in excellent detail in Chic Scott's *Summits & Icefields: Canadian Rockies*, it is unnecessary to repeat the descriptions here. I do offer, however, some supplementary words of wisdom to snowshoers. All Wapta ascents are rated "mountaineering," and the requisite skills and gear are mandatory for anyone trying these ascents. With the exception of Mount Jimmy Simpson, all of the trips involve

ABOVE: On the way to Crowfoot Mountain. BELOW: A typical snowshoeing position when you do Wapta ascents as day trips. St. Nicholas, Olive and Gordon can be seen in the background.

glacier travel, and you should rope up – even though the majority of skiers on the Wapta go unroped. Skis do distribute one's weight better than snowshoes do, so skiers may feel they can get by on these ascents without ropes, but I certainly wouldn't recommend it. Crampons and an ice axe are essential for several of the trips. Also, note that the canyon on approach to the Bow Hut is a classic terrain trap. Don't go near it without a beacon, probe, shovel and several friends to dig you out should the terrain above the canyon let loose.

## Mountains of the Wapta Icefield

For fantastic scenery and views you simply can't go wrong with any ascent on the Wapta, and I highly recommend *all* of the following trips. All times are for day trips and all routes are via the Bow Hut approach as described by Chic Scott, unless otherwise noted. Pertinent maps for these trips are 82 N/9 Hector Lake, 82 N/10 Blaeberry River, and Gem Trek Bow Lake and Saskatchewan Crossing.

### Crowfoot Mountain
10–12 hours; recommended as a day trip.

### Mount St. Nicholas
11–13 hours; snowshoe to the St. Nicholas/Olive col and then go on foot to the summit; crampons and ice axe required; possibly some rope work near the summit.

### Mount Olive
See Mount St. Nicholas; can be combined with an ascent of St. Nicholas. Allow 14-17 hours for both Olive and St. Nicholas.

### Mount Gordon
12–14 hours; the least steep of the ascents; snowshoe all the way to the summit.

### Mount Rhondda
13–15 hours; steep for only one short section; snowshoe to the summit.

### Mount Thompson

13–15 hours; ascend via the southwest slopes; some avalanche hazard; snowshoe to the summit.

### Mount Jimmy Simpson

8–10 hours; no glacier travel but steep avalanche slopes must be ascended.

# Snowshoe Ascents on the Columbia Icefield

The peaks of the Columbia Icefield are some of the tallest the Canadian Rockies have to offer. The scenery on and around the icefield is awe inspiring, and the views from the summits are utterly breathtaking. Like trips to the peaks of the Wapta, the overwhelming majority of ascents in this area are completed on

SASKATCHEWAN GLACIER BELOW AND THE COLUMBIA ICEFIELD TO THE UPPER LEFT. NOTE THE ANGLE OF THE SLOPE TO THE LEFT — DEFINITELY IN THE AVALANCHE POTENTIAL RANGE.

AT skis. Naturally this makes them potential snowshoe ascents. However, because of the length and seriousness of these routes, snowshoes are an impractical method of ascent. Nevertheless, the possibilities are still there for the most diehard snowshoe mountaineers. Only Castleguard, Andromeda and Snowdome are possible as day trips (brutally long days). All others require at least two, and in most cases three, days of travel.

The Athabasca Glacier provides the shortest access to all peaks on the Columbia Icefield except for Castleguard Mountain. This glacier is also the most serious obstacle in the area to overcome. Though benign-looking from the toe and when snow-covered, the glacier is riddled with enormous crevasses, especially around the two icefall areas that must be ascended. Roped parties of three or more are strongly recommended. Travelling only

*DESCENDING CASTLEGUARD MOUNTAIN
WITH SNOWSHOES ON THE BACKPACK.*

with one other person could be deadly should one of the party fall into a crevasse. Extricating an injured person from a crevasse by yourself is extremely difficult and in some cases impossible. Serious incidents and fatalities have occurred on this glacier, and with continued glacial recession it is likely the number and severity of those incidents will increase.

Again, see Chic Scott's *Summits & Icefields: Canadian Rockies* for detailed route descriptions. All the trips noted below for this area are rated "mountaineering" and require you to bring avalanche equipment and glacier travel gear.

The Columbia Icefield is prone to long stretches of bad weather and the accompanying whiteouts. Navigation in a whiteout can be very dangerous. Wait for a high-pressure system to arrive before you venture onto the icefield. Take plenty of sunscreen.

# MOUNTAINS OF THE COLUMBIA ICEFIELD

If I only had time to try three of the following trips, I would choose Castleguard, Andromeda and North Twin. Maps for these trips are 82 C/3 Columbia Icefield and Gem Trek Columbia Icefield.

## Castleguard Mountain

16–19 hours; a straightforward and relatively safe ascent on the icefield but requires a great deal of energy; access is via the Saskatchewan Glacier.

## Snowdome

14–18 hours; the rounded summit means you have to walk around the summit area for about 30 minutes to take in all of the view.

## Mount Andromeda

14–18 hours via the southwest ridge; fantastic summit view.

## Mount Columbia

Two very long days (approximately 12 hours each) or three shorter, but still long, days (approximately 8 hours each).

## North Twin

Three very long and exhausting days (approximately 12 hours each); I'm told the summit view is unparalleled.

## The Stutfields

Three long days (approximately 10 hours each); similar to Snowdome in their rounded summits.

# Appendix B: Snowshoeing Creeks and Frozen Lakes and Creeks

## Creeks

Snowshoeing up and/or alongside various creeks is sometimes a good way to salvage bad-weather days. Often the scenery around a creek is not as spectacular as it is on trips that gain significant elevation, and so the view on creek trips will be secondary, perhaps, to exercise. Some of the creeks mentioned here wind a long way up a valley. You can make your day as long or as short as you like. In the early season, snowshoes may not even be necessary.

The following is by no means an exhaustive list of all the creeks in the Canadian Rockies that would make enjoyable snowshoe trips. These trips do, however, offer a good starting point. All except King Creek are straightforward, with very little avalanche hazard.

1. Porcupine Creek on Highway 40 south: park on the side of the road, about 17 km south of the Trans-Canada, where Porcupine Creek (signed) runs under the highway; snowshoe in a southeast direction.

2. Wasootch Creek on Highway 40 south: park at the Wasootch parking lot, about 19 km south of the Trans-Canada, and hike southeast along the very wide and dried-up creek bed. A short distance in, take note of the popular climbing routes on Wasootch Slabs, on the north side of the creek.

3. King Creek on Highway 40 south: park at King Creek parking lot, about 50 km south of the Trans-Canada, and snowshoe east along the creek. This enormously popular ice-climbing destination is very scenic but it does have some avalanche hazard; take the necessary precautions.

4. Cougar Creek in Canmore: from Highway 1A, turn onto Elk

Run Blvd. and park in the paved lot by Cougar Creek bridge; the creek runs in a northeast direction.

5. Exshaw Creek in Exshaw: from Highway 1A, turn in to Exshaw and park in the small lot by Exshaw Creek; snowshoe or hike north, on the west side of the creek.

6. Jura Creek near Exshaw: on Highway 1A, park at the side of the road opposite the "Graymont" sign, about 1.5 km east of Exshaw. Snowshoe (or more likely hike, given the eastern location of the creek) north up the creek; a scenic canyon is soon reached. If the canyon is impassable, bypass it high on the left bank. Return to the creek and continue north.

7. Noseeum Creek on Highway 93 north: park at the pull-off on the north side of the road, about 23 km north of the Highway 1/Highway 93 junction. Parking may be inaccessible because of snow. Head northeast, enjoying the impressive scenery around Mount Andromache and "Noseeum Mountain."

## Frozen Lakes

There are a number of large lakes in the Rockies that make worthwhile snowshoe destinations in themselves. Travel is usually easy (obviously, because lakes are flat!) and generally safe at the right times of the year. The best time to go out onto a frozen lake is between mid-December and April. However, an unseasonably warm autumn or spring might encroach on those times and discretion and caution should be used. January, February and March are almost guaranteed to be safe (if global warming is okay with that for now). Remember, when snowshoeing on lakes, it is important to be aware and considerate of ice fishers.

A lake's elevation is an important factor in determining how soon in the season it freezes. At a low elevation of approximately 1400 m, Barrier Lake may not be safe for travel until January or even later. In contrast, Spray Lake, sitting at an elevation above

1800 m, can be frozen to a depth of over a metre by mid-December. Keep this in mind if you are planning to take an early-season excursion onto a frozen lake.

The south end of Spray Lake is my favourite of the lake trips, boasting terrific views of the surrounding mountains and interesting ice, which you can see when it is blown clear of snow. I recommend the following lakes as snowshoeing destinations:

1. Spray Lake: North end access from anywhere along Highway 742 from the Spray Lakes Campground turnoff to several kilometres south of the Spray Lakes parking lot; South end access from the Shark Mountain parking lot (see Mount Fortune for route description, page 169).

CHECKING OUT THE ICE ON THE SOUTH END OF SPRAY LAKE. CONE MOUNTAIN IN THE BACKGROUND.

2. Lower Kananaskis Lake: access from the Lower Lakes parking lot along Kananaskis Lakes Trail.
3. Upper Kananaskis Lake: access from either the North Interlakes day-use parking lot or the Upper Lake parking lot; both near the end of Kananaskis Lakes Trail.
4. Lake Minnewanka: access from the Lake Minnewanka parking lot, off the Trans-Canada, near Banff.
5. Bow Lake: access from the Bow Lake pull-off, a few kilometres west of the Crowfoot Glacier pull-off or the Num-Ti-Jah parking lot; both on Highway 93 north.
6. Waterfowl Lakes: access from pull-offs alongside the northern lake, just northwest of the Waterfowl Lakes Campground, on Highway 93 north.

ICE AND SNOW COVER BOW LAKE, THE STARTING POINT FOR CALGARY'S DRINKING WATER. PLEASE DON'T PEE IN THE LAKE!

# Appendix C: Trips Organized by Level of Difficulty

The following lists are designed to assist you in picking objectives appropriate to your skill level, knowledge, experience and goals for a specific day. Note that the majority of trips in this guidebook are classified as intermediate and do require avalanche gear.

## Easy/Beginner Trips with Limited Views

These trips are good ones to take when the weather is not good. You'd do these primarily for the exercise and the enjoyment of being in the mountains.

Don't expect any mind-blowing vistas!

- 36. Warspite Lake, page 214
- 39. Sawmill Loop, page 223
- 47. Stoney Squaw Mountain, page 249
- 48. Tunnel Mountain, page 251

## Easy/Beginner Trips with Good Views and Little to no Avalanche Hazard

Like the previous suggestions, these trips will appeal to beginner and intermediate snowshoers, but they are better done on good-weather days to best enjoy the views. In general, no avalanche gear or additional equipment (crampons, ice axe) will be required.

- 3. "Carthew Minor" (to Summit Lake only), page 88
- 4. Forum Ridge, page 92
- 9. Bull Creek Hills (excluding the Fir Creek descent), page 118
- 11. Junction Hill, page 127
- 16. Read's Ridge, page 146
- 19. North Ridge of Mount Buller (to ridge only), page 155

## Intermediate Trips with Avalanche Hazard

Don't go into these areas without avalanche gear and the requisite training and knowledge. If the avalanche hazard is "considerable," use discretion and common sense, and always err on the side of caution. If the avalanche hazard is "high" or "extreme," **do not** go on these trips. Mountaineering experience is strongly recommended. Good views are almost guaranteed on each trip if the sky is clear.

## Advanced Trips with Avalanche Hazard and/or Glacier Travel

These trips are only for those with mountaineering experience. Avalanche gear, crampons and ice axe are mandatory. A rope and snow/ice anchors may also be needed.

## Extremely Strenuous Trips

Trips in this category will push the physical limits of even the fittest people. Know what you are in for if you do any of these routes as day trips, and be prepared to suffer a little or a lot! Some people might question their inclusion in this book as day-trip ascents, but my brother and I did them as such. Of course, there is almost always the option to split the ascent over two or more days.

# Appendix D: Trips Not Described in this Book

The following trips are either already popular snowshoe destinations or have the potential to be popular and/or exciting trips. I have not completed any of them on snowshoes and therefore cannot give specific route descriptions (except Cascade Amphitheatre, but that was a very long time ago). The official snowshoe trails in Kananaskis are terrific for beginners and anyone who wants an easy and hazard-free day out. Maps and route descriptions are readily found on the Internet for those routes.

## Elbow Valley

1. Prairie Mountain

## Kananaskis

1. Elk Pass (official snowshoe trail)
2. Village Loops (official snowshoe trail; same starting point as for Mount Kidd Lookout)
3. Penstock Loop (official snowshoe trail)
4. Canyon (official snowshoe trail)
5. Lower Lake (official snowshoe trail)
6. Marsh Loop (official snowshoe trail)
7. Elkwood Loop (official snowshoe trail)

## Highwood (before December 1)

1. Ptarmigan Cirque
2. Arethusa Cirque/Little Arethusa
3. Elbow Lake and Rae Glacier
4. Mount Lipsett
5. Nameless Ridge

## Banff

1. Cascade Amphitheatre
2. Boom Lake
3. Bourgeau Lake
4. Taylor Lake
5. Tower Lake and/or Rockbound Lake (Highway 1A, near the Castle Junction turnoff)

## Lake Louise

1. Lakeshore Trail
2. Lake Agnes/The Beehive
3. Plain of Six Glaciers
4. Mount Fairview (**serious avalanche danger**)
5. Moraine Lake Road
6. Paradise Valley Trail

## Yoho

1. Ross Lake
2. Paget Peak Lookout

## Highway 93 North

1. Wilcox Pass

ON THE RIDGE ABOVE CASCADE AMPHITHEATRE,
LOOKING AT MOUNT CASCADE.

# Bibliography

Connally, Craig. *Mountaineering Handbook: Modern Tools and Techniques That Will Take You to the Top*. Camden, Me.: Ragged Mountain Press, 2005.

Daffern, Gillean. *Gillean Daffern's Kananaskis Country Trail Guide, Volumes 1, 2*. Calgary: Rocky Mountain Books, 2010 (vol. 1), 2011 (vol. 2).

Daffern, Tony. *Backcountry Avalanche Safety for Skiers, Climbers, Boarders and Snowshoers*. 3rd ed. Calgary: Rocky Mountain Books, 2009.

Dougherty, Sean. *Selected Alpine Climbs in the Canadian Rockies*. Calgary: Rocky Mountain Books, 1999.

Ferguson, Sue A., and Edward R. LaChapelle. *The ABCs of Avalanche Safety*. Seattle: The Mountaineers Books, 2003.

Fredston, Jill A., and Doug Fesler. *Snow Sense: A Guide to Evaluating Snow Avalanche Hazard*. 4th ed. Anchorage: Alaska Mountain Safety Center, 1999.

Graydon, Don, and Kurt Hanson. *Mountaineering: The Freedom of the Hills*. 6th ed. Seattle: The Mountaineers Books, 2001.

Jamieson, Bruce. *Backcountry Avalanche Awareness*. Revelstoke, BC: Canadian Avalanche Association, 2000.

Kane, Alan. *Scrambles in the Canadian Rockies*. 2nd ed. Calgary: Rocky Mountain Books, 2003 (3rd printing, 2011).

Potter, Mike. *Ridgewalks in the Canadian Rockies*. 2nd ed. Airdrie, Alta.: Luminous Compositions, 2009.

Scott, Chic. *Ski Trails in the Canadian Rockies*. 3rd ed. Calgary: Rocky Mountain Books, 2001.

———. *Summits & Icefields: Canadian Rockies*. Calgary: Rocky Mountain Books, 2003.

# Index

Andrew Nugara was born in Rugby, England, and moved to Canada in 1979. He earned bachelor degrees in Music Performance and Education from the University of Calgary and presently teaches high school mathematics in Calgary, Alberta. In 2001 he discovered the magnificent Canadian Rockies, and since then he has completed over 300 mountain ascents.